Praises For

Come Away with Me

Janice Rigel is a woman after God's heart. I love seeing her courageous love for Jesus throughout social media and believe a 50 day devotional is another beautiful way for her to point us all to Jesus. May everyone who puts their hands to this devotional encounter His loving kindness and the real Jesus we read about in the bible.

—Jamie Lyn Wallnau
Author of Holy Revolution and Host of the Set Apart Podcast

***

Janice is truly a joy! Not only do these devotions speak truth and impart strategies for walking in the freedom our loving Heavenly Father intends, but the questions also prompt each reader to pull back the layers of beliefs and expectations to explore our true identity in Christ. That identity is so much more than what the world will tell you is yours! Read each devotional entry and meditate on the truth within. Soak in it and let it wash away the spiritual grime and leave you refreshed in His presence!

—Keri Kitchen, MEd, LPCC, NCC
The Every Day Royalty Podcast

***

The *Come Away with Me* devotional brings the reader to new depths in their relationship with the Lord. Each page features God's word and brings it to life in an engaging and digestible way. I love that the devotional also contains applicable prayers that the reader can speak over their life. Pure, true and powerful! Every believer will want this devo in their rotation!

—Katie Hedrick
Certified Christian Life Coach and Host of the Stepping Into a Joy Filled Life Podcast

***

Janice has cultivated in these pages an enriched outlook on what a relationship with God is truly intended to look like. Reading this devotional inspired a fresh perspective on what it means to be lost in the fullness of the Lord and invoked a desire to draw nearer to Him.

—Tiffany Elaine Conn
Worship Pastor at Freedom Church Clarksville.

***

I love that Janice shares the same passion I have to pursue intimacy with God, to revel in his mad love for us, and to truly know Him and make Him known. There is no better way to live than to abide in Him through prayer, worship, and His Word, and it is through abiding that we learn to recognize and trust His voice speaking directly to us. This devotional is a wonderful way to tap into golden nuggets of truth that will aid in that abiding. It will connect you with God every time you pick it up and draw you into a deeper relationship with Him. Abide in Him, my friend. "For in Him we live and move and have our being." - Acts 17:24

—Jenna Dexter,
Christian Life Coach
TotalThrive.com

***

God is calling His sons and daughters to draw close to Him in the secret place, so they may be filled with His power and walk in His authority. To draw closer in intimacy requires us to put

aside the busyness of life, silence the noise around us and actively learn to listen to our Father's voice. Janice gives us an unbelievable tool to do just that. Your life will be transformed as you daily dive into each scripture enriched devotional. Allow these daily readings to draw you further into the secret place with God, because in the secret place is where you will find peace, joy and wisdom for your life. God is enough my friend!

"Taste and see that the Lord is good; blessed is the one who takes refuge in Him." (Psalm 34:8 NIV)

—Jennifer Elston
Pastor - Holland First Assembly
Conference Speaker

***

As Christians we tend to think our God is a man up there that is hard to communicate with. We tend to build our relationship with Him around religious beliefs that we have been taught or picked along the way.

This book opens your eyes to what it means to have an intimacy with OUR GOD who is A FATHER and A FRIEND.

—Lucy Blessed
Writer and Blogger
Founder of The One Grateful LEPER

Come Away with Me

*Cultivating Intimacy
in the Secret Place*

JANICE RIGEL

Published by KHARIS PUBLISHING, imprint of KHARIS MEDIA LLC.

Copyright © 2021 Janice Rigel

ISBN-13: 978-1-63746-083-2
ISBN-10: 1-63746-083-X

Library of Congress Control Number: 2021950380

All rights reserved. This book or parts thereof may not be reproduced in any form, stored in a retrieval system, or transmitted in any form by any means - electronic, mechanical, photocopy, recording, or otherwise - without prior written permission of the publisher, except as provided by United States of America copyright law.

All Scripture quotations, unless otherwise indicated, are taken from the Holy Bible, the NEW KING JAMES VERSION®. Copyright© 1982 by Thomas Nelson, Inc.

Used by permission. All rights reserved.

All KHARIS PUBLISHING products are available at special quantity discounts for bulk purchase for sales promotions, premiums, fund-raising, and educational needs. For details, contact:

Kharis Media LLC
Tel: 1-479-599-8657
support@kharispublishing.com
www.kharispublishing.com

This book is dedicated to every passionate lover of Jesus that has impacted my life and previous generations of believers who paved the way for mine. To my neighbors growing up who would take me to church, to every VBS, Sunday school teacher, and minister of the gospel who planted seeds of faith in me throughout the years, thank you. Your seeds are bearing fruit. To my pastors, Matt and Pete, who have always encouraged me to read, know and love the Bible, and communicated that intimacy with God isn't just for select people. It's for everyone. To my mentors, Jessica and Cindy, who have poured wisdom into my life and shown me what it looks like to love God with all of my heart, soul, mind, and strength. Thank you for the many conversations, for correcting me when I need it, for your prayers, and for your presence in my life. To my mom, dad, and sisters for filling my life with laughter and encouraging me to chase my dreams - I love you!

TABLE OF CONTENTS

Day 1	Lavish Love	1
Day 2	Withholding Nothing	3
Day 3	Pour It Out	5
Day 4	Speak Lord	8
Day 5	Known	11
Day 6	Always More	14
Day 7	Satisfied	17
Day 8	Banner of Love	19
Day 9	Reveal	21
Day 10	Shut the Door	23
Day 11	Seen	25
Day 12	Abide	27
Day 13	Dwell	30
Day 14	Hidden	33
Day 15	Unrestricted	36
Day 16	Fullness of Joy	39
Day 17	Bask Away	42
Day 18	Unabandoned	44
Day 19	Removing Expectations	47
Day 20	Ablaze	50
Day 21	Refreshed	53
Day 22	Purified in His Presence	56
Day 23	Refuge	58
Day 24	Consumed	62
Day 25	Treasure	64
Day 26	Costly	67
Day 27	Delight	70
Day 28	Seek	73
Day 29	Shine Brightly	76

Day 30	First Love Intimacy	79
Day 31	Radiant	84
Day 32	Behold	87
Day 33	Inescapable	90
Day 34	Faithful Love	93
Day 35	Vast	96
Day 36	Ask See Knock	99
Day 37	Come Home	102
Day 38	Silence	105
Day 39	Searched	108
Day 40	Holy	111
Day 41	Breakthrough	114
Day 42	Sow in Tears	117
Day 43	Access	120
Day 44	Kindness	123
Day 45	Thankfulness	126
Day 46	Measure the Distance	129
Day 47	Truth	132
Day 48	Steadfast	135
Day 49	Wholehearted	138
Day 50	Come Away with Me	141

Lavish Love

"See what great love the Father has lavished on us, that we should be called children of God! And that is what we are!" -1 John 3:1a NIV

The way God loves is always lavish. Lavish means "bestow something in generous or extravagant quantities on." His love is unchanging, unwavering, and without measure.

The generous and extravagant love of God is not like we experience in any other relationship. The fact that the God of all creation wants a relationship with us is inexplicable and overwhelming. I heard someone say once that God peers through galaxies to look upon us. So many other things could captivate His attention, yet He chooses to fix His focus on us. What a thought!

I echo the words of David in Psalm 8- *"who am I that you are mindful of me?"* Who are *we* that God is mindful of us? I cannot understand why such a mighty, powerful, all-knowing God would want anything to do with frail, broken, sin-bent humanity, but I am beyond thankful that He does.

You have a Heavenly Father who stops at nothing to prove His lavish love for you. Romans 5:8 tells us that "God demonstrates His own love for us in this: While we were still sinners, Christ died for us." God did not wait for us to "get it right" or to do something to earn His love. No price could be paid that would suffice the sacrifice Jesus made to display His love at the cross. He freely gave Himself and continues to every moment of every day.

The two greatest commandments God gives us are to love Him with all of our being and to love others as ourselves (Mark 12:30-31). We love because He first loved us (1 John 4:19). The world will know that we belong to God by our display of love (John 13:35). We may be a fraction of a speck of dust amongst the vast sum of creation, yet He chooses to love us. Let's model His great love to a lost, broken, and hurting world that desperately needs to know that there is a God in Heaven who lavishly loves them, too.

Ponder verses: John 1:12, John 10:18, Romans 8:32

Prayer:
Heavenly Father, thank You for Your lavish love and for stopping at nothing to prove Your love to me. Thank You for Your display of love at the cross and for all that You sacrificed for me. I am so thankful to be called Your child. I pray that I would live my life from a place of strong identity in You. I pray that You would reveal more of Your great love to me. Help me to love You and love others lavishly. In Jesus' name, amen.

Withholding Nothing

"For the Lord God is a sun and shield; the Lord will give grace and glory; no good thing will He withhold from those who walk uprightly" -Psalms 84:11 NKJV

When we walk uprightly, God promises to withhold no good thing from us. Walking uprightly does not mean that we are perfect. If that were the case, none of us would receive anything from Him because none of us are perfect. Walking uprightly means that we are walking in relationship with Him.

Having a relationship with God gets vastly over complicated in explanation and application. It is over-complicated because we make it about what we can do, which makes our relationship indicative of our behavior or good works. We don't fall in and out of relationship with God as if He is some sort of revolving door. Good works are always a product of relationship, not a prerequisite.

When we know Him intimately and read and apply His Word, we can't help but be changed. Let all that you do be an overflow of knowing Him, rather than a way of trying to earn right standing. Do you spend time with Him because you feel like you *have* to, or do you spend time with Him because you *want* to? Ask yourself the same question regarding reading His Word, gathering with other believers, sharing His truth with those around you, and all other things that you "do" in life as a means to glorify and serve Him.

We must understand that our relationship with Him isn't based on our good deeds but on a choice to love and live for the God who already loves us endlessly. 2 Peter 1:3 tells us that God gives us everything we need for life and godliness. Over and over, scripture affirms that there is nothing that we need that God will not provide.

Do we give our all to the God who continually gives His all to us? Are there areas of our lives that are not fully surrendered to Him? My prayer is that as we examine our own lives, there would not be one thing that we withhold from Him. He deserves it all.

Ponder verses:
James 1:17, Matthew 6:25-34, Psalm 34:10

Prayer:
Heavenly Father, thank You for providing all of my needs and even blessing beyond that with my wants. You are Jehovah Jireh, my Provider. I trust that all that I need is found in You and that You withhold no good thing from me. God, I don't want to withhold anything from you. Show me any area of my life that I have not fully surrendered to You. I want to give all that I am to You. In Jesus' name, amen.

Pour It Out

"And behold, a woman in the city who was a sinner, when she knew that Jesus sat at the table in the Pharisee's house, brought an alabaster flask of fragrant oil, and stood at His feet behind Him weeping; and she began to wash His feet with her tears, and wiped them with the hair of her head, and she kissed His feet and anointed them with the fragrant oil." -Luke 7:37-38

An unnamed woman only referred to in scripture as "a sinner" learned of Jesus' whereabouts and unashamedly entered a home filled with religious leaders to pour out her most valuable possession, an alabaster flask of fragrant oil. She washed His feet with her tears and wiped them with her hair. She kissed His feet and anointed them with the fragrant oil.

No words were spoken as her extravagant act of love and intimacy was on display for a room full of critical people and later recorded in scripture to be countlessly retold for the rest of all time. Such an audacious move for such a low-esteemed woman, yet she boldly made her move anyway. She laid aside her pride, cultural expectations, fear of man, and anything else that would hold her back from giving Jesus her all.

The heaps of insults and disapproval that those present indignantly hurled at her were met by the mercy of Jesus. While others accused her, He defended her. While they called her "sinner," He called her "forgiven." While others were repulsed, He was redeeming. While others were protesting, He blessed her with peace.

How often do we feel unnamed, unwanted, and unimportant? Our mistakes, inescapable reputation, and undesirable parts of our past slap labels on us, and we wonder if anyone knows our actual name. I promise you that the One who created You not only loves you, He wants You, and He knows your name.

Jesus told those present that this woman loved Him much because she had been forgiven much. Is our display of love towards God congruent with the forgiveness and mercy He has shown us? What is your alabaster flask? What do you have of value that you can "pour out" at His feet as a display of your love for Him?

Ponder verses: Luke 7:36-50

Prayer:
Heavenly Father, thank You for calling me by name and loving me the way that You do. Thank you for meeting me in my mess and showing me immeasurable mercy. I pray that I would display a love for You like the woman with the alabaster flask; that I would care more about showing You my love than I would about what those around me think. God, I pour all that I am at Your

feet because I love You, and You are worthy of all that I am. In Jesus' name, amen.

Speak Lord

*"The **LORD** came and stood there, calling as at the other times, "Samuel! Samuel!" Then Samuel said, "Speak, for your servant is listening."*
- 1 Samuel 3:10

God has spoken to His people throughout all of history, and He still speaks to us today. He has things that He wants to communicate to us, and one of the benefits of knowing Him is the ability to hear and recognize Him when He speaks. John 10 says that we as His followers know His voice and that we will not follow the voice of a stranger.

His Word, the Holy Bible, is always our fixed point of reference. Anytime we feel like we are hearing from God, it must line up with the Word of God. If what we hear doesn't, then we can know with certainty that it is *not* God's voice we are hearing.

Samuel was dedicated to the Lord by his mother Hannah and ministered under the high priest Eli at the house of the Lord in Shiloh. He lived in a time when "the word of the Lord was rare" (1 Samuel 3:1). The Holy Spirit had not yet been given to God's people (fast forward to the New Testament for that). Hearing God speak was not a common or frequent occurrence. Samuel heard a voice calling to him three times, each time mistaking it as the voice of Eli. Finally, after going to Eli the third time, Eli told him that it must be God speaking and to respond by saying, "Speak, for your servant is listening."

God was calling to Samuel because He had something to say to him (you can read the complete account in 1 Samuel 3). God calls to us for the same reason because He has something that He wants to communicate to us. You can hear God for yourself. You do not need another person, or a "mediator," to speak to God for you or to deliver a message from God to you. Yes, God uses people to relay messages, and I thank God for that, but God wants to speak directly to *you* at times as well.

What is our response when God speaks? Do we go about our days with our spiritual ears covered, or are we open to hearing Him speak? I pray that our response to His speaking would be like Samuel's - "speak, for your servant is listening."

Ponder verses: 1 Samuel 1:21-28; 1 Corinthians 3:16; Acts 7:48

Prayer:
Heavenly Father, thank You for speaking to me. I pray that my spiritual ears would always be open to hearing Your voice. I want to be so familiar with Your voice that I don't dismiss or mistake it as anyone else's. I thank You for giving me Your Word and that You always speak to me through it. As I hear You speak, I also pray that I would be obedient to whatever it is You speak

to me. Thank You for the boldness and courage that You give me. In Jesus' name, amen.

Known

"Not everyone who says to me, 'Lord, Lord,' will enter the Kingdom of Heaven, but only the one who does the will of my Father who is in Heaven. Many will say to me on that day, 'Lord, Lord, did we not prophesy in your name, and in your name drive out demons, and in your name perform many miracles?' Then I will tell them plainly, 'I never knew you. Away from me, you evildoers!'"
- Matthew 7:21-23 NIV

One of the most sobering verses in all of scripture is Matthew 7:23. Jesus tells us that only those who do the will of God will inherit the Kingdom of Heaven and that those He does not know will be told to depart from Him. This is a harsh truth that is not easy to read and not popular to teach, yet we must take into account all of God's Word, not just the parts that our itching ears want to hear (2 Timothy 4:3). All of His Word is truth, and we don't get a pass because of ignorance or preference.

The people mentioned in these verses are those who did a lot of good works in His name, yet the reality is that it was all done outside of a personal relationship with Him. We cannot forsake intimacy and connection with God for faith-stamped accomplishments. Endeavors outside of a relationship with Him are not worth it. It's important to remember that our good works are not what get us saved; it is only by His grace, our confession, and our belief in Him (see ponder verses below).

How do we know His will for our lives? His Word confirms His will for all of us, and His voice confirms His will for us personally. There are concrete things in scripture that are across the board applicable to all people, such as forgiveness, rejoicing, prayer, giving thanks, sanctification and salvation. Then there are things that the Word does not explicitly detail that we can only know by hearing His voice for ourselves, such as what job to take, who to marry, where to live, etc. God has good plans for all of our lives, and we can know them by reading His Word and being open to hearing His voice.

Let all that you do be done in love (1 Corinthians 16:14). My motive in sharing the verses in today's devotional is to encourage you to be intentional with your relationship with God. Doing great exploits in His name isn't worth sacrificing knowing Him and being known by Him. Spend time with Him in prayer. Read His Word. Bask in praise and worship. Then let all that you do to impact the world *for* Him be an overflow of that intimacy.

Ponder verses: John 17:3; Ephesians 2:8-9, Romans 10:9, 1 Thessalonians 4:3 & 5:16-18

Prayer:
Heavenly Father, thank You for the truth found in Your unchanging Word. Thank You for the ability to know You and to

be known by You. God, I ask that You fill me with a desire to abide in relationship with You more than anything else. Let my life never be about good works as a means to earn Your love, but rather an overflow of intimacy with You. In Jesus' name, amen.

Always More

"Now to Him who is able to do exceedingly abundantly above all that we ask or think, according to the power that works in us, to Him be glory..."
- Ephesians 3:20-21a

God is not lacking, running on fumes or scratching His head, wondering how to do anything. He is never unsure of how He can and will meet the needs and even wants of His people. He possesses all that we will ever need - physically, emotionally, mentally, and spiritually.

He is not a God of scarcity; He is a God of more than enough. Whenever we are presented with a need and are tempted to doubt God's faithfulness to supply, we can remind ourselves of 2 Corinthians 9:8-*God is able to make all grace abound toward you, that you, always having all sufficiency in all things, may have an abundance for every good work.*

In all four gospel books, we read about Jesus preaching to the multitudes and the miracle of the multiplication of bread and fish. Scripture records that an estimated 15,000 people showed up because they recognized Him and His followers. They came by the droves, knowing fully well Jesus' reputation for healing and performing miracles.

The Bible tells us that Jesus had compassion for the people and healed those who were sick. While wonderfully miraculous, it was probably expected because they knew that's what He did. It's what they came for, but Jesus didn't stop at that. He took a few fish and loaves of bread, blessed them, and made sure everyone present had plenty to eat.

I love that Jesus was into showing both extravagant and practical displays of God's love. He showed the massive crowd compassion by healing them, and then He fed them dinner. He went above and beyond what the people asked for or imagined that He would do. He saw a need (hunger), and He met it.

There is no need that God will not meet, and He promises in Ephesians to do exceedingly abundantly above all that we ask or think. He wants to show His favor and provision in all areas of our lives. He doesn't just barely unclench His fists to give us what we need; He goes above and beyond with wide open hands. He is a God who blesses us extravagantly, who knows what we need, and always gives us more.

Ponder verses: Philippians 4:19; Matthew 14:13-21

Prayer:
Heavenly Father, thank You for being a generous God. I thank You that You do exceedingly abundantly above all that I ask or think. All that I need is found in You. You are a miracle-working God, and You are still doing miracles today. I lay aside all

doubt and worry, trusting that You will always give an abundance for every good work. In Jesus' name, amen.

Satisfied

"You open Your hand and satisfy the desire of every living thing." - Psalm 145:16

The promise of derived desires is fastened to the premise of first delighting ourselves in Him (see Psalm 37:4). When we find the satisfaction of our soul in knowing God and having an intimate relationship with Him, we can trust Him to simulate the desires of our heart with His.

There is a woman whose story is told in John chapter 4. While traveling with the disciples from Judea to Galilee, Jesus took a route through Samaria that Jews typically avoided. The Samaritans were viewed as unclean by the Jewish people, and the hostility was mutually reciprocated. There was much animosity and avoidance between the Jewish and Samaritan people, so for Jesus, a Jew, to travel through Samaria defied and broke social and cultural expectations.

Not only did they travel through Samaria, but they stopped there to take a break. The disciples went in search of food while Jesus rested by Jacob's well. A woman came along to draw water, and Jesus sparked up a conversation by asking her to give Him a drink. She was taken aback that a Jewish man would be talking to her, and her response was to remind Him that she was a Samaritan woman. To remind Him that He should not be talking to her.

Jesus ignored her remarks and continued the conversation by describing Himself as the source of living water and eventually revealing Himself as the Christ. He tells her that when we drink natural water, we eventually become thirsty again, "but whoever drinks of the water that I shall give him will never thirst" (verses 13-14). The result of her encounter with the only One who can truly satisfy the thirst we have was an eagerness to bring others in her community to Jesus. When they met Him, they also believed and said, "we know that this is indeed the Christ, the Savior of the world" (verse 42).

We all have a thirst that can only be satisfied by Christ, the source of living water. The world offers a lot of misleading mirages that will only leave us dehydrated. Every desire and every thirst is met in Him. He is not clenching His fists towards us; His hands are wide open to satisfy our every desire.

Ponder verses: Psalm 37:4, John 4:1-42

Prayer:
Heavenly Father, thank You for always meeting me right where I am, just like You did with the Samaritan woman. Help me identify and remove any mirages of the enemy and saturate my life with the living water. Thank You for satisfying every thirst that I have with Your truth. I want every desire of my heart to align with Yours. In Jesus' name, amen.

Banner of Love

"...his banner over me was love." - Song of Solomon 2:4b

God has placed a banner of love over each of us.

1 Corinthians chapter 13 is known as the love chapter in the Bible and details what love is and isn't. I want you to ask yourself if the words that describe love are what you're allowing to wave like a banner over your life.

Love is *patient, kind, not envious, not boastful, not proud, not rude, not self-seeking, not easily angered. It keeps no record of wrong, does not delight in evil, rejoices in the truth, always protects, always trusts, always hopes, always perseveres, never fails.*

Many of us have proverbial banners waving over us that were not designed by God. Those banners could say a myriad of things - *unwanted, unloved, not good enough, hopeless, ugly, stupid, hated, mistake, forgotten*. Any banner with words on it that contradict what God's Word says about us is a lie and needs to be removed from our lives. We must choose to only stand under the banners that He puts over us.

I want to hone in on verse 6 of the love chapter, which says that love "rejoices in the truth." So often, we are deceived into thinking that if truth causes offense or discomfort, then it is more loving to say nothing. I could not disagree more. We are instructed in Ephesians 4:15 to "speak the truth in love." Love doesn't passively refuse to confront uneasy situations. Love's ammunition isn't avoidance; its arsenal is truth.

The Word of God is our pivot-point and fixed point of reference for truth (see John 17:17). We must know what the scriptures say, apply them to our own lives and then respond to others with truth laced in love.

What messages are on the banners that are over your life? Are they reflective of the heart of God, or are they more in alignment with the ways of the world? My prayer is that you let His banner of love supersede and replace all other banners as you live your life rejoicing in His truth.

Ponder verses: Proverbs 3:3, 1 John 4:8, 2 Corinthians 10:5, 1 Corinthians 13

Prayer:
Heavenly Father, thank You for placing a banner of love over my life. God, I ask for Your help to identify any banners that have been placed over me either by other people, the world, or even myself, that are not what You say about me. I ask that every lie be replaced with Your truth. Help me to always speak Your truth in love to myself and to others. In Jesus' name, amen.

Reveal

"The secret things belong to the Lord our God, but those things which are revealed belong to us..." - Deuteronomy 29:29a

God has countless things that He longs to reveal to His children. He wants to share His heart and character, assure us of who we are in Him, communicate His plans, and divulge details regarding the world we are living in. There are precious experiences only acquired within the secret place, such as the awakening of dreams and desires, heavenly visions and interpretations, specific prayer strategies, and clear direction for our lives.

We were created to communicate with our Creator. We can share what's on our hearts with Him and also know that it's ok to ask questions. So many of us have been programmed to believe that God is unapproachable and that He doesn't have time to answer our seemingly unimportant questions. Neither is true.

The Word tells us that we can come into His throne room boldly. We don't have to wait for an invitation from Him; He has already invited us in. Don't reserve that invitation for "in case of emergency"; He is always willing and waiting for you to come. Go into the throne room of God because you love Him. Go into the throne room of God because you want to spend time with Him. Go into the throne room of God because that is where you find your answers. He is your source of strength, help, grace, mercy, provision, security, rest, and all other things.

When we spend time with the Lord, we need to ask Him for wisdom and discernment regarding the details of what He shows us. There are aspects of the secret place that are, and only ever will be, just between Him and us. There will also be times when God will show us something or speak a word that is meant to be shared, possibly with someone specific and at other times with many. Allow Him to lead and give direction in those regards.

We find the truth within His Word and within His presence. He has much on His heart to share with ours, but do we make space in our lives to allow Him to do so? Do we take time to hear from Heaven and let God reveal His truth to us? He is more than willing to meet us in the secret place, so let's determine to meet Him there frequently.

Ponder verses: Hebrews 4:16, John 16:13

Prayer:
Heavenly Father, thank You for giving me access to Your presence. I know that I can boldly come before You. I say "yes" to Your invitation to intimacy. All that I need, and will ever need, is found in You. God, I ask that You reveal anything about Yourself or my life that You want to. I want to know You more and live a life of truth. In Jesus' name, amen.

Shut the Door

"But you, when you pray, go into your room, and when you have shut your door, pray to your Father who is in the secret place; and your Father who sees in secret will reward you openly." - Matthew 6:6

As the tumultuous noise of the world continues to get louder, there is a deep urgency for believers to "shut the door" and spend time praying to the Father. We cannot afford to abandon the secret place and to skate through life solely on pre-dinner and bedtime prayers. There is a very real spiritual war being waged, and it is time for us to engage.

In our hustle and hurry, busy-stricken culture, it can be so easy to unintentionally avoid the place of intimacy where His presence resides. We must be willing to confront distractions and remove anything that hinders us from spending time with Him. Not only does He desire that for us, but we desperately need it.

There is a time and space for corporate prayer, and that is crucial and must not be neglected. We need to gather with other believers to pray with and for one another, but there must also be a consistent, vibrant time that we spend alone with the Lord. Just Him and us, one-on-one, behind "closed doors." These are the moments that He refreshes us personally, speaks truth to our hearts, shows us of things to come, ministers to us individually, and, most importantly, is the time we get to just bask in His presence and spend time with Him.

The reward is seen openly, but it is never what we strive for. We spend time in the secret place because we desire intimacy with Him. We intentionally carve out that time in our schedules so that we can make being with Him a priority. The time we spend with Him affects all other areas of our lives. It's where we find the answers we need to important questions and life decisions. It's where we find healing and wholeness. It's where our identity is affirmed, and our strength is found.

Schedule time with Him, and don't let anything hinder it. When I spend time with Him, I often imagine Him sitting in a chair across from me, forehead to forehead, holding my hands. In those times, it's important that we not only share our hearts but that we leave space for Him to share His. He has things to say to us, and it's time to shut the door and pray to our Father in the secret place.

Ponder verses: Jeremiah 33:3; James 4:8

Prayer:
Heavenly Father, thank You for reminding me of the value of spending time in the secret place with You. I ask for wisdom to lay aside distractions and make being with You my top priority in life. I want to share my heart, and I want to hear what's on Yours. In Jesus' name, amen.

Seen

"O Lord, You have searched me and known me."
- Psalm 139:1

There is something equally freeing and frightening about being fully exposed. When everything is laid bare, and nothing is left to hide, we can feel simultaneously liberated and vulnerable. Our Creator has seen the deepest parts of who we are; the places and spaces we may have kept completely hidden from others are not hidden from Him. Nothing escapes His gaze.

He sees it all and still chooses to love us.

Throughout scripture and the entire course of human history, we see evidence of His unfailing love towards humanity. In the book of Genesis, God is revealed as "El Roi," commonly translated to "the God who sees me."

His loving eye is on the grieving, the hopeless, the hurting. His loving hand is continually outstretched, ready to lift the lost and fallen. His loving voice is relentlessly wooing people into a deeper place of intimacy with Him.

There is no pain we go through, a joy we celebrate, or a mundane moment of our lives that He isn't fully aware of. He wants to be actively involved in all aspects of our lives, but many shelf Him as an "in case of emergency-only" kind of God. When life is good, we often forget He exists and fail to realize our constant need for Him. Oppositely, many shelf Him when times get tough, accusing Him when things go wrong. We question His goodness and ability to lead our lives. Both are dangerous traps.

We have to stay steadfast and know that He is Lord of all, in the good times and in the difficult times of life. He wants to navigate us through all seasons of life, continually keeping His promise to work all things together for our good (Romans 8:28). We must become so deeply confident in His unchanging character that we are unmoved by the circumstances of our lives. When times get tough, we praise Him. When times are good, we praise Him. Nothing is hidden from the God who sees all.

Ponder verses: Psalm 32:8; Psalm 139

Prayer:
Heavenly Father, thank You for seeing me exactly where I am and for loving me enough to find me, heal me, and redeem me as Your own. Thank You for searching me and knowing me. You are the God who sees me, and Your gaze is always on me. God, I invite You into every area of my life and trust Your leading through every season that I walk through. I want You to be Lord of all the good and the difficult times in my life. I choose today to trust Your leading and stay steadfast in You. In Jesus' name, amen.

Abide

"I am the vine, you are the branches. He who abides in Me, and I in him, bears much fruit; for without Me you can do nothing." - John 15:5

Many are searching for answers that can only be found in Him. We are in a fruit frenzy, scrambling for those things. Galatians 5 tells us that the Holy Spirit gives us love, joy, peace, patience, kindness, goodness, faithfulness, gentleness, and self-control. In our current culture, the word "choose" is frequently slapped onto the front of many of those words listed-choose joy, choose love, choose kindness. Instead of trying to "choose" the fruit of the Spirit, we should choose Jesus, and then from that place, the fruit will be given to us.

The fruit the world offers us is both fleeting and counterfeit. I imagine it as perfectly appealing to the eye, yet seedless and rotting within. We look for peace in promotions, love in relationships, joy in accomplishments, and self-control from within our own strength. There are not enough self-help books, motivational speeches, or social media memes that can "will us" to fruitfulness.

We can't produce fruit on our own, and we can't find fruit outside of a relationship with Him.

We find fruitfulness by abiding within the vine (Jesus). The fruit He grows in us is spiritual, long-lasting, and benefits our own lives as well as the lives of those around us.

Verse 7 of John 15 says, "If you abide in Me, and My words abide in you, you will ask what you desire, and it shall be done for you.". What a promise for answered prayers! But, His words must abide, or remain, within us. We want and need fruit that is persistent and unswayed by what is happening in our lives and the world around us. When we are connected to Him, He is our source of all things pertaining to life and godliness (2 Peter 1:3).

Why bear fruit? The answer is found in verse 8 of John 15 – "by this, My Father is glorified, that you bear much fruit." He not only wants us to bear fruit, He wants us to bear *much* fruit.

Our fruitfulness - living a life filled with love, joy, peace, and all of the other fruits - brings glory to our Heavenly Father. My prayer is that our lives will bring much glory to the God of glory as a result of our desire and willingness to abide in Him.

Ponder verses: John 15:1-8; Colossians 3:16; 1 John 4:16

Prayer:
Heavenly Father, thank You for the ability to abide in relationship with You. God, I want Your words to dwell in me richly and for my life to glorify You in every way. I know that this

world has nothing for me and that all that I am searching and longing for is only found in You. I desire to abide in You and for Your words to abide in me. Prune me so that I can bear much fruit for You, Lord. In Jesus' name, amen.

Dwell

"He who dwells in the secret place of the Most High shall abide under the shadow of the Almighty." - Psalm 91:1

The shadow of our Almighty God is a place of refuge and protection. Dwelling in the secret place of the Most High is key to abiding under the shadow of the Almighty.

Psalms 91 gives many promises to those who dwell (live) in the secret place:

- Refuge and fortification in Him
- Deliverance
- A shield of truth
- Fearlessness
- Protection from evil, enemy arrows, and pestilence
- Angelic protection
- Answers when we call upon Him
- Honor
- Long life
- Salvation

Dwelling in the secret place isn't something we stop and start. It's a place of unrelenting continuation.

It's a place we adamantly refuse to leave. It's a place we firmly resolve to stay in no matter what.

Our faith and relationship with God should have integrity. It must look consistent, regardless of the environment we are surrounded with. We aren't called to display the life of a believer only within the confines of a church building. Our lives during a church service should look no different than our lives the rest of the week. Are we the same person at home and at our secular jobs as we are when we are surrounded by other believers? Or is our character like a chameleon - adapting to our surroundings?

My prayer is for a resilient body of believers who are consistent in character, confident in who they are in Christ, and know what it means to dwell in the secret place perpetually.

Ponder verses: Psalm 17:8; Psalm 36:7; Psalm 91

Prayer:
Heavenly Father, thank You for being my refuge and hiding place. My protection, deliverance, and provision are found in You. I commit all of my days to dwell in the secret place with You. Thank You for Your presence that surrounds me and is within me. There is not a place that I go that You have not already gone before me. I trust the path You have laid out for me and am grateful that You never leave or forsake me. In Jesus' name, amen.

Hidden

"your life is hidden with Christ in God" - Colossians 3:3b

So many distractions plague our lives and vie for our attention and affections. The world is full of lures to keep our focus on the temporal and diverted from eternity. We are bogged down with concerns regarding our jobs, finances, families, hobbies, and day-to-day demands of life. While those things are important, they can easily become idols, stealing our fidelity from the One who matters most.

The Lord spoke to my heart recently to "stay hidden" in Him. As culture becomes increasingly corrupt and confusion, chaos, and contention escalate all around us, it's crucial that we stay steadfast in our pursuit of the things He has called us to and not get caught up in the cares of this life. The enemy would love for us to spend our time pursuing pointless endeavors that are not even a part of God's purpose for our lives. The effects are exhaustion and burnout, as well as missing out on what God actually has planned for us.

Jesus perfectly modeled what it meant to live a life totally surrendered to the will of the Father. Even from the young age of twelve, He declared His purpose was to be about His Father's business (Luke 2:49). His surrender to abandon all for the cause He was sent for was then modeled in the lives of His disciples, who left all they knew to follow Him. For three years, they traveled, ministered, and did life with Jesus.

What does it look like to live our lives abandoned to the Lord? So many of us are reluctant to answer the call of God because we are afraid that we won't like what that looks like. Apprehension causes us to hesitate giving our full "yes" to God. We live below all He has for us because we are stopped by fear - fear of the unknown, fear of man, and fear of failure.

I want to encourage your heart with confidence in the Lord. He promises to equip us for everything that He calls us to (2 Timothy 3:17 & Hebrews 13:21). There is nothing that He will ask us to do that He will not go before us and be with us while we do it. We must remember that it's never about us; it's always about Him. I pray that we become passionate about knowing Him and making Him known, living abundant lives as we remain hidden in Him.

Ponder verses: Psalm 27:5; Galatians 2:20; Colossians 3:2

Prayer:
Heavenly Father, thank You for the purposes and plans that You have designed for my life. Thank You for the ability to live my life hidden in You. I want to be about my Father's business, living my life in a way that honors and glorifies You in all that I do. I pray against anything that keeps me from living fully in

all that You have for me. I trust that You are ordering my steps and that Your Word illuminates the path before me. Have Your way in all areas of my life. In Jesus' name, amen.

Hidden Poem

When I feel overwhelmed, and life is just too much
When my aching heart is heavy, Jesus, You are enough

You are the rock I run to, my forever firm foundation
You're the Creator that I cling to without fear or hesitation

When I'm weary and heavy laden, You give the rest I need
When chaos is consuming, You are the perfect peace

You're the still inside the storm, the calm in the commotion
You're the truth in times of trouble; You set miracles in motion

When life seems uncertain, and I don't know what to do
You are the Way of Wisdom; my hope is in Your truth

When my focus is fixed on You, my soul stays satisfied
You're my healer, my protector, the shelter where I hide

You bear every burden and lift every load I carry
You break every chain; You give strength when I'm weary

Your Word will sustain me while You're making all things new
My life is hidden in You Jesus, and my heart belongs to You

Unrestricted

"Let us, therefore, come boldly to the throne of grace, that we may obtain mercy and find grace to help in time of need." - Hebrews 4:16

A beautiful thing happened the day that Christ gave His life on the cross. *"Then, behold, the veil of the temple was torn in two from top to bottom; and the earth quaked" (Matthew 27:51).*

The veil hung outside the innermost, most sacred space in the temple known as the Holy of Holies, a space that was virtually off-limits. The only one permitted to enter into this area of the temple was the high priest, and only once a year to offer incense and sacrifices for the sins of the people.

When the veil, a very thick and (humanly) impossible to rip curtain, was torn, it symbolized the unrestricted, open access believers were granted to boldly and confidently enter into the presence of God from that time on. We no longer have to wait to enter His presence. We no longer need someone to go before God on our behalf.

The Spirit of God that once dwelled in the Holy of Holies now resides within believers. If you belong to Him, His Spirit lives within you. That thought alone is worth spending time frequently to ponder. Romans

8:11 says that "the Spirit of Him who raised Jesus from the dead dwells in you." If this is true, which the Word of God always is, then our lives should reflect this. We should expect things to happen when we pray, for atmospheres to change as a result of His presence within us, and for our homes, workplaces, churches, and communities to be directly affected by the fact that believers are present (even if it's only you).

What should we do with this unrestricted access that we are given to the presence of God? We know His Spirit dwells within us, and we know we have access to go before the throne of grace boldly. I want to encourage and remind you that the presence of God is accessible anywhere and at all times. He is not restricted to your church building, a certain time of the week, or to your pastor and church leadership. If you are a follower of Christ, then you have access to Him 24 hours a day, 7 days a week, anywhere that you find yourself - in your home, at the grocery store, in your car, at your workplace. His unrestricted presence goes everywhere that you go because you carry Him with you.

Ponder verses: Acts 17:24; 1 Peter 2:9

Prayer:
Heavenly Father, thank You for sacrificing Your Son, Jesus, so that I can have a restored relationship with You. I thank You that nothing stands in the way any longer from Your presence-You have given me full, unrestricted access to Yourself. My heart

is Your home, and I want to live my life in a way that demonstrates the incredible power of Your Spirit that is alive and well within me. For all of my days, I live to glorify You. In Jesus' name, amen.

Fullness of Joy

"In Your presence is fullness of joy" - Psalm 16:11 (partial)

Whenever I hear someone say they lack joy, my first response is to encourage them to get into His presence. The Word tells us in Psalms 16 that in His presence is not only joy but the fullness of it. So the solution to a lack of joy is to find ourselves in His presence.

For some, spending time in His presence looks like taking a walk in nature. For others, it can look like climbing into their closet (literally) and getting alone with Him. For me, I love to get in my car and drive or put on music and sit on the floor in my living room. Other times I will go to the hill behind my church with a blanket and my Bible. Being intentional is everything. Setting aside the time and space to spend time with just Him is something He desires, and we need.

We have the opportunity to spend our time doing many things, but spending time with Him is what we need most, just like Mary, who chose to sit at Jesus' feet instead of helping her sister Martha. The Lord's response to Martha's complaints about the lack of help was, "Why are you upset and troubled, pulled away by all these many distractions? Are they really that important? Mary has discovered the one thing most important by choosing to sit at my feet. She is undistracted, and I won't take this privilege from her." (Luke 10:41-42 TPT)

How we hang out with God can look different day-to-day or in different seasons of life. God isn't boring or monotonous, so our relationship with Him shouldn't be either. Make it fun, like you would any relationship. Think outside the box.

Experiencing His joy in our everyday lives is possible. It doesn't mean that we are ignorant of the problems of this world or that we stick our fingers in our ears and pretend like everything is perfect. It does, however, mean that despite what is going on around us, we can have peace and joy within us and firm confidence and trust in the One who holds the entire world in His hands (Psalms 95:4).

Grab your Bible and a journal and find creative ways to spend time with Him. Get into His presence because that's where you will find the fullness of joy.

Ponder verses: Acts 2:28; Romans 15:13

Prayer:
Heavenly Father, thank You for the freedom and fullness of joy that I find within Your presence. God, I pray that my relationship with You would never become mundane or lackluster. I know that my relationship with You is the most important relationship that I will ever have. I want to know You more than I do and to never grow stagnant in my faith. Lord, I ask You to

inspire my heart with creative ways to spend time with You. I want my time with You to be meaningful and enjoyable. In Jesus' name, amen.

Bask Away

"Be still, and know that I am God" - Psalm 46:10a

Hearing the words "be still" often connotes the idea of silence and stagnation. While there is value in surrendered silence and deliberately making space to settle your heart and hear from the Lord, the stillness God is instructing us to do in Psalms is much deeper than just being quiet.

In Hebrew, being still means to let go and cease striving.

It's time for us to let go of things that hinder us and hold us back from doing, seeing, and being all that God has purposed and created us for.

Hebrews 12:1 tells us, *"Let us lay aside every weight and the sin which so easily ensnares us, and let us run with endurance the race that is set before us."* This verse makes it clear that two things can hold us back from running our faith race well: sin and weight.

Allow God continual access to search your heart and be diligent to guard it well. I truly believe we can live our lives free from sin entanglements by staying in constant fellowship with the Lord, addressing sin quickly, repenting, and walking in grace. Just because we may sin doesn't mean we have to stay stuck in it. Acknowledge it, repent and move on.

Weights are anything that holds us back. I imagine them as burdens on our backs or weights around our feet that prevent us from moving as quickly as we could be. Weights could look like lies we have believed, pains from our past, and mistaken identity (not fully realizing who we are in Christ).

I am prophesying that today will be a day that you find complete freedom in all areas of your life and that you will be freed from ALL sin and weight; that you will not be ensnared in any way, and that you will be able to run your race with passion and endurance. Nothing is stopping you, tripping you up, or holding you back anymore, in Jesus' name.

What are some areas of your life that you need to "let go and stop striving"? Take time to bask in His presence and allow the Lord to search your heart and reveal the answer to that question.

Ponder verses: Ephesians 2:10; Proverbs 4:23

Prayer:
Heavenly Father, thank You for the ability to hear Your voice. God, I ask You to search my heart and show me any area that I need to let go of and stop striving. I want to live my life with freedom and victory in every way. In Jesus' name, amen.

Unabandoned

"He will not leave you nor forsake you."
- Deuteronomy 31:6b

One of the last things Jesus spoke before ascending to Heaven after the resurrection was a faithful promise to always be with us (Matthew 28:20). He knew that we would always need Him, and so He sent His Holy Spirit to be our Comforter, Advocate, Helper, Counselor, and so much more. He promised to give us a Helper to abide with us forever, the Spirit of truth (John 14:16-17), and He keeps every promise He makes.

There is a call to God's people to not abandon the secret place. We need personal time with the Lord to become a priority in our everyday lives. God not only has things He wants to communicate to us, but He also simply just wants to spend time with us.

How do we ensure that we don't abandon that much-needed time? I believe the answer is found in abandoning anything that hinders us from making space for the Lord. Ask the Lord for wisdom concerning what you need to lay down in your schedule to make that happen. If we are too busy for the Lord, we are too busy.

This doesn't mean that we cease to live our everyday lives and avoid responsibilities and obligations. It does, however, mean that we begin to carefully examine those things that fill our schedules and pull our attention away from what matters most. Much of what we classify as important really has no significant eternal value and only serves as a source of distraction.

In the Gospel books of the New Testament (Matthew, Mark, Luke, and John), the story of the disciples reflects what it means to truly forsake all to follow Him (see Luke 5:11). They left all that they knew - their families, careers, and communities - to follow Jesus. They had no idea what they were signing up for and quickly realized that the price they paid would cost them everything. It wasn't a cheap sacrifice to make, but it was worth it. When Jesus pointedly asked them if they would abandon Him, Peter's response was like anyone who has truly experienced a relationship with the One true God - "Lord, to whom shall we go? You have the words of eternal life.". Peter knew there was no one and no place more worthy of allegiance.

Make a promise to not abandon time with the God who promises to never abandon you.

Ponder verses: Psalm 94:14, Hebrews 13:5; Colossians 3:1

Prayer:
Heavenly Father, thank You for Your promise to always be with me. Thank You for sending the Holy Spirit to always be with

me and to be my Counselor, Advocate, and source of truth. I know that You keep every promise that You make. Help me to live my life according to Your truth and to never be too busy to make spending time with You a priority. I ask for wisdom to focus on what is eternal and what really matters. In Jesus' name, amen.

Removing Expectations

But as it is written: "Eye has not seen, nor ear heard, nor have entered into the heart of man the things which God has prepared for those who love Him." - 1 Corinthians 2:9

The Lord is not moved by our Spirit-less agendas and man-made timeframes, ideas, methods, and formulas. Religion teaches us to attempt to formulate God, but His ways are higher (Isaiah 55:9) and cannot be contained within the walls of our human limitations.

We often expect Him to move in ways we have heard about in the past or ways we have personally experienced Him. We cannot limit our expectations by comparing what He is doing presently with what He has done in the past. He is an "I'm doing a new thing" kind of God. All He does will always line up with His Word, but the way He moves is never monotonous.

Diving into the gospel accounts of the life of Jesus, specifically regarding the way He healed the blind, will prove that His methods are anything but methodical. In Matthew 9, Jesus touched the eyes of two blind men, and they received their sight. In Mark 10, He simply spoke a Word to a man named Bartimaeus, and his eyesight was restored. In John 9, Jesus spit in the dirt, made mud, and rubbed it on a blind man's eyes. All three completely different approaches; all three equally as powerful.

Just as He operated in unordinary ways by demonstrating His power and love through healings, He also wants to move in astounding ways as we spend time seeking Him in the secret place. We must let go of our expectations and the ways we think He should move and let Him move according to *His own* will and the way He wants to.

Don't limit Him.

God has unique experiences that He wants to share with just you. Be enamored with the aspect of surprise. Make the plea of your heart be, "God, I don't know what you have for me, but I want it." Trust that all that He has for you is and only ever will be good. We must hear His voice and move according to His Spirit. It's time to believe Him for the more and to remove our limiting expectations.

Ponder verses: Isaiah 43:19; Luke 1:37

Prayer:
Heavenly Father, I am so thankful that You are not a cookie-cutter kind of God. Thank You for the thrill and joy of seeking and serving You. I trust that Your plans for me are, and only ever will be, good. I know that You have new things that You want to do in and through my life, and I say "yes" to You, God. I lay down all of my selfish motives and relinquish my desire to

be in control. I pray for an increase in expectation and a renewed desire to know You more. In Jesus' name, amen.

Ablaze

"A fire shall always be burning on the altar; it shall never go out." - Leviticus 6:13

Many question if they'd be willing to die for their faith. While most of us will never face the reality of martyrdom, we are daily confronted with the decision to live for Him amidst an unbiblical, ungodly culture. As New Testament believers, we are called "living sacrifices." This means that while we live, we live for Him.

The Bible calls believers "temples of the living God" (1 Corinthians 3:16). His Holy Spirit lives within us (Romans 8:11). After the resurrection of Christ and the coming of the Holy Spirit, God's presence became accessible in ways previously unheard of. No longer does His presence dwell in temples made of human hands (Acts 7:48 & 17:24); His presence now resides within us.

Our hearts and lives are portable altars. Wherever we go, He goes.

His holy fire burns within our hearts and can be likened to one of three different types of fire. Ask the Lord to examine your heart to see which one defines your current heart-fire status.

The first is like a fire that is barely burning; embers are glowing, and the fire is near going out. It has been squelched by disappointment, loss of hope, and cares of this world. The second is bright and blazing but confined and contained. It functions within the realm of safety, comfort, and predictability. The third and final fire is like a raging forest fire. It is uncontained, uncontrolled, and unrelenting. It burns everything within its path and causes everything that gets near it to be consumed. This is a fire filled with passion and intensity that cannot be quenched.

The Bible tells us that in the last days, the love of many will grow cold (Matthew 24:12). My prayer is that the fire on the altar of our hearts will never go out. I believe God is calling all of us to a place that reflects the third fire; being completely captivated and consumed by Him. I believe His Spirit is stoking the flames of our internal fires so that we burn brightly and live lives that are completely ablaze for Him.

Ponder verses: Romans 12:1; Romans 14:8; Galatians 2:20; 1 Corinthians 6:20

Prayer:
Heavenly Father, I ask You to fan the flame within me and help me to burn brightly for You. God, I want my life to glorify You. I pray that my love for You will never grow cold but will only ever increase in intensity. Examine my heart and remove anything that is preventing me from burning brightly. I want a fire within me that is not contained and that affects everything surrounding

me every moment of every day. You are all that matters, and I choose to live my life for You. Thank You for keeping me ablaze. In Jesus' name, amen.

Refreshed

"Come to me, all you who are weary and burdened, and I will give you rest." - Matthew 11:28 NIV

Weariness is plaguing our hearts and minds, our communities, and our culture.

Weariness is defined in 2 ways:
1. Extreme tiredness; fatigue
2. Reluctance to see or experiences any more of something

Weariness is a persistent enemy attempt to stop the call of God on our lives, or at the very least delay or muddy it. So many believers are living on the precipice of completely giving up - on their dreams, on the promises God has given them, on the fullness of God's best for their lives. Even unintentionally, we allow weariness the right to remove what is rightfully ours as co-heirs with Christ. We forfeit without a fight.

One woman's story is highlighted in Matthew, Mark, and Luke. She was a woman who undoubtedly knew what it meant to be weary. For twelve years, she suffered from a medical condition that caused her to bleed continually. She exhausted every effort to find healing, and scripture tells us that she not only suffered at the hands of many physicians, she also grew worse.

Outside of the miraculous, her situation was utterly hopeless.

When Jesus came to her town, she refused to forfeit the opportunity to come to Him. In a culture that told her to hide away because she was deemed "unclean," she boldly stepped out instead. Her faith told her that "if only I may touch His clothes, I shall be made well" (Mark 5:28). Pressing through the multitude of people thronging Jesus, she came from behind and touched the hem of His garment, and immediately she was healed. She purposed to press in, and the outcome of her faith was exactly what she needed - healing.

So what is the antidote for weariness? Jesus gives us the clear answer in Matthew 11:28 - to come to Him! The refreshing, healing, and wholeness we need can only be found in Him. If you find yourself in a season of spiritual weariness, relinquish everything to come to Him because He is where deep, lasting refreshing is found.

Ponder verses: Matthew 9:20-22; Mark 5:25-34; Luke 8: 43-48; Acts 3:19

Prayer:
Heavenly Father, thank You for inviting me to come to You when I am weary and heavy-laden. I know that You will give me the rest that I need and that in Your presence, I will be refreshed. God, I ask You to move in every area of my life that has been bombarded with weariness, and I pray life into those seemingly

dead places. You are the God who refreshes, resurrects, redeems, and restores. I trust You with every weary place in my heart and life, and I choose to press into Your presence no matter what is happening around me. In Jesus' name, amen.

Purified in His Presence

"No flesh should glory in His presence" - 1 Corinthians 1:29

The presence of God is a place that the flesh loses its power. The flesh is anything - mindsets, actions, motives - that is contrary to God's best for us. We can know His best for us by knowing His Word, character, and truth given through His Word. His presence purifies us from the flesh and makes us more like Him.

What happens in His presence?

-Fullness of joy (Psalm 16:11)
-Freedom (2 Corinthians 3:17 and Galatians 5:13)
-Minds are renewed (Romans 12:2)
-True identity is found (2 Corinthians 5:17)
-Purpose is revealed (Jeremiah 29:11)
-Chains are broken (Psalms 107:14)
-Strongholds are pulled down (2 Corinthians 10:4)

The Word attaches promises to encountering His presence. When we draw near to Him, He promises to draw near to us (James 4:8). When we seek Him, He promises to be found (Jeremiah 29:13). When we call out to Him, He promises to save us (Romans 10:13). He is already standing at the door (of our hearts and lives), knocking (Revelation 3:20), but it is our choice whether or not we open the door and let Him in.

If our lives are not aligned with His Word, we cheapen what He paid for us at the cross. The Bible says that Jesus came to reconcile us to God and give us abundant life (Romans 5:10 and John 10:10). When we live our lives according to the flesh, we live beneath abundance. Abundance looks like thriving in our relationship with Him, bearing fruit, and continually growing in our faith.

We are called to walk according to the Spirit and not to gratify the lusts of the flesh. This world will always attempt to allure us to lower standards and temporary pleasures and pursuits, but God is continually calling us to live our lives from a place where we are purified in His presence, continually being conformed to the image of Him (Romans 8:29).

Ponder verses: Psalm 51:7-17; Galatians 5:16-25; Ephesians 2:6; 2 Peter 3:18

Prayer:
Heavenly Father, thank You for the gift of Your presence. I ask You to meet me right where I am and to expose and remove anything in my life that is not pleasing to You and that isn't Your best for me. Purify me in Your presence and make me more like You. I surrender completely to You and choose to walk according to the Spirit. In Jesus' name, amen.

Refuge

"God is our refuge and strength, a very present help in trouble." - Psalm 46:1

Refuge: *a condition of being safe or sheltered from pursuit, danger, or trouble; something providing shelter*

The Bible describes God as our refuge, shelter, fortress, and strong tower. Even if we find safety nowhere and in nothing else, we are always safe with Him. He is our unfailing, fortified retreat from the cares and scares of this world.

The secret place of His presence is not just for a select few. As Jesus journeyed the earth, He persistently invited others into close proximity with Him - the lame, the lepers, the sick, the outcasts. No one was untouchable to Him. Not only did He welcome people to "come to Him", but He also pursued them when they had no way to get to Him on their own.

In Matthew 8, Mark 5, and Luke 8, we read about a demon-possessed man who encountered Jesus. He was bound in torment, naked, living in a graveyard, and cutting himself with stones. He was so violent, he was unapproachable - but by God Himself. Jesus set the man free from the demons, clothed Him, and restored his mind. This man became a missionary to a region of ten cities (Decapolis), sharing the good news of what

Jesus had done in his life and impacting many. Jesus pulled him into a place of freedom and deliverance, and his life was eternally changed.

Jesus is still inviting all to experience the haven of His heart, the place where His glory dwells, and shame, fear, and worry are eradicated by His love. As we find our refuge in the God of all creation (Colossians 1:16), we have the ability to become a safe haven for those around us. God is calling us to be people who invite others into the protected place we are abiding in through Christ, as well as pursue those around us with the good news of the gospel.

Are people safe in our presence? Are we a "safe place" for others to confide in without the fear of gossip, slander, backbiting, and criticism? Do people leave us feeling defeated and torn down, or built up and encouraged? The second greatest commandment is to "love others as ourselves." If we have found our reprieve in God, why wouldn't we want that for others? Let's tell the world that there is real refuge and shelter in our God.

Ponder verses: Psalm 91; Proverbs 18:10; 2 Corinthians 2:20;

Prayer:
Heavenly Father, thank You for being my safe place of refuge. Thank You for delivering me and setting me free. God, show me how to love others as myself and be a safe haven for them. I ask for boldness to share the gospel and to share the good news of what

You have done in my life. Use me to change the world. In Jesus' name, amen.

Refuge Poem

My soul's lover, my most intimate friend
My perfect peace, beginning, and end

My ever-present help in times of trouble
My holding hand when life crumbles

My firm foundation beneath my feet
My shelter from storms and rock of retreat

My protection and salvation, the One I seek
My courage and strength when I am weak

My champion defender, my heart's delight
My valiant warrior in every fight

My stronghold of hope, my shield, and horn
My redeemer and savior when weary and worn

My fortress and my gift of grace
My refuge and my hiding place

Jesus

Consumed

"Our God is a consuming fire" - Hebrews 12:29

Consuming: *completely filling one's mind and attention; absorbing*

Scripture is filled with reminders of the reality of God's consuming love for us. Psalm 139 tells us that His thoughts toward us outnumber the grains of sand and that He is intimately acquainted with us. Take a moment to settle that truth into your heart. He is always for you, not against you, and His plans for your life are only ever good.

God is so consumed with you that He created you, demonstrated His love for you at the cross, persistently pursues you, and desires to do life with you day in and day out. He isn't just a "Sunday morning" kind of God; He is a 24/7, 365 days a year kind of God. He wants to be a part of your life every moment of every day.

Is the burning desire that God feels towards you one that you reciprocate?

Recently I attended a conference, and during worship, the Lord spoke to my heart about the reality of being consumed by Him. He reminded me that before Jesus came as the ultimate sacrifice for sins, animal sacrifices had to be made on an altar (check out the Old Testament for more in-depth details). Those sacrifices were consumed by fire. As God's people, we are called to be living sacrifices (Romans 12:1), consumed by the fire of the Holy Spirit.

In Matthew 3:11, John the Baptist tells those in his midst that Jesus will baptize "with the Holy Spirit and fire." By diving into the book of Acts, we can see the beginning fulfillment of that spoken Word, and Jesus is still baptizing His followers with the Holy Spirit and fire today. This baptism ignites boldness within us and helps us to live a life of holiness.

I encourage you to ask the Lord for the Holy Spirit's baptism and fire. Let's purpose in our hearts to be consumed by the God who is already completely captivated with us; to burn with a fiery love that is so bright within us that the lost, hurting, and broken world we live in can't help but be changed.

Ponder verses: Psalm 139; Jeremiah 29:11; Romans 8:31

Prayer:
Heavenly Father, I ask You to ignite in me a fire that burns brightly for You. Consume me with Your presence and power. I choose to let my light shine brightly. I want to affect the world around me with Your truth. God, I remove the limits I have put on You and give You permission to move in and through me as You want. In Jesus' name, amen.

Treasure

"Lay up for yourselves treasures in Heaven...for where your treasure is, there your heart will be also " - Matthew 6:20-21

Where are you laying up your treasure? By paying attention to where we daily fix our focus, we can find the answer to that question. It's not difficult to examine our lives and see where we are laying up our treasure. Our pursuits and ambitions indicate how we are spending our lives - whether for this world or Heaven.

Our heart will settle on wherever we choose to store up our treasure. It is a choice we get to make. Proverbs 4:23 tells us that out of the heart "spring the issues of life." This means that everything regarding our life stems from what is going on within our hearts - the way we think, the way we act, the way we speak. What life is your heart storing up treasure for - this temporary life or eternal life?

If our treasure is in this world, a very fleeting existence, then we will spend our time, energy, and money on things that are temporal. James 4 describes our life as "a vapor"; it "appears for a little time then vanishes away." Whatever we do that does not have eternal value is wasted. The Bible says that this is treasure that can be stolen or destroyed.

If our treasure is in Heaven, our eternal existence, then we will spend our time, energy, and money on things that are everlasting. This looks like investing in the lives of other people and loving them the way Jesus instructs us to, reading and applying the Word of God, sharing the Good News of the Gospel, and most importantly, walking in relationship with God. The Word says that this is treasure that cannot be stolen or destroyed.

We can't have double-vision; our gaze cannot be on this world and on eternity simultaneously. Jesus made it very clear we can only either be *for* Him or *against* Him. It's both feet in the world or both feet in the Kingdom; we can't straddle the line. We must make a choice.

I encourage you to spend your lives for what is lasting and what truly matters - eternity. Make knowing Him your first and greatest passion in life. Press into Him for what your life's purpose is, and then spend yourself doing everything He has created you to do. Give your time, money, and attention to what is everlasting, and store up your treasure in Heaven.

Ponder verses: Proverbs 4:23; James 4:4; James 4:14

Prayer:
Heavenly Father, thank You for giving me the ability to store up treasure in Heaven that cannot be stolen or destroyed. God, I know this life is temporal, and I want to live my life with an

eternal perspective. Have Your way in and through my life. In Jesus' name, amen.

Costly

"So likewise, whoever of you does not forsake all that he has cannot be My disciple." - Luke 14:33

To give up everything to gain everything is a perfect paradox of what it means to live for the Kingdom of God. Jesus demonstrated a life lived in total surrender to the will of the Father. He willingly gave His life (John 10:18) so that we could have a reconciled relationship with God, something that was previously impossible due to sin and the fall of humanity.

Romans 5:1 tells us that we have "peace with God through our Lord Jesus Christ." This peace is not a fuzzy-feeling state of mind. It's a bridge-gapped between God and us by the blood that Jesus shed at the cross. It was such a costly sacrifice that just knowing the painful path He would be taking caused Jesus sheer agony in the Garden of Gethsemane (read Luke 22 for the details). Yet, despite what it took, Jesus still chose obedience to the plan of laying down His own life because He saw what would be gained by it - you!

When speaking to His followers, Jesus did not sugar-coat the price they would have to pay to follow Him. He did not promise them a better earthly existence in exchange for their allegiance. He promised them persecution, being misunderstood and even hated. He made it clear that if they didn't forsake all, they couldn't even be His disciple. Most of His first disciples died of martyrdom and endured much for the sake of the gospel, yet their lives served to advance the Kingdom, and their reward is in Heaven.

God does not ask for half-hearted allegiance; He requires an all-in commitment. We cannot be medial believers - it's all or nothing with God. But the beauty is that when we give Him our entire selves, He promises to give us something better - life. *For whoever desires to save his life will lose it, but whoever loses his life for My sake will find it - Matthew 16:25.*

One of my favorite quotes is by Jodie Hughes, someone I deeply admire in the faith:

"I knew this call would cost us everything, but everything is no sacrifice at all in service to the living King." Living for God may be costly, but it's entirely worth it. When we truly know God's heart for us and that He is the source of life itself, whatever we must surrender to wholly follow Him will be insignificant compared to living for the Author of life itself.

Ponder verses: Mark 8:36; 1 Corinthians 6:20; Hebrews 12:2; 1 John 2:15-17

Prayer:
Heavenly Father, thank You for willingly giving Your Son Jesus to die on the cross for me. Thank you for making a sacrifice so costly so that I could have peace with You and walk in relationship with You every moment of every day. I ask You to reveal

any area of my life that I have not fully surrendered to You. Whatever it costs, God, I choose to live for You. I lay down my life for Your sake, knowing that only in You will I find true life. In Jesus' name, amen.

Delight

"The LORD, your God, is with you, the Mighty Warrior who saves. He will take great delight in you" - Zephaniah 3:17

If you were asked to imagine what God looks like and explain it, what would you say? How would you describe His countenance? Stoic and serious? Happy and joyful? A bit of both?

It's nearly impossible for many to imagine that the sovereign God of all creation could have a smile on His face. Yet, many scriptures paint a picture of God depicted by delight. Spiritual fruits (Galatians 5), including joy, are a display of Who He is. Viewing God as happy does not eliminate His majesty and holiness; it actually magnifies it.

He takes great delight in you, and He rejoices over you with singing!

The song He continually sings over you is a good song. I often contemplate what He is singing over me. I know it's a song saturated in love, peace, and delight because I know that He takes great pleasure in His people. When we see Him as distant, stoic, and serious, it can create a disconnect and cause us to put up walls. It's difficult to desire drawing near to a God that is portrayed as unapproachable.

But that's not Who He is. Because of Jesus, we can boldly approach the throne of the One who takes great delight in us (Hebrews 4:16).

The meaning of the word 'delight' includes captivate, joy, happiness, and gladness. We can confidently know He takes great delight in us because His Word tells us He does. Do we take that same delight in Him? Psalms 37:4 says to "make God the utmost delight and pleasure of your life" The word delight in this passage means "to be soft or tender." Are we soft and tender to His voice and His ways? Are we captivated by Him? Are we passionate about His presence?

God doesn't want us to just live our lives for Him; He wants us to live our lives *with* Him. To wake up every morning knowing that He has purposes within the day ahead. To allow Him to speak to us throughout our day and lead our lives, even in the mundane moments that are seemingly insignificant. To let Him use us to impact the world and let others see that our delight is found in a God who sees His creation, us, and takes great delight.

Ponder verses: Psalm 40:8; Psalm 119:16; James 4:8

Prayer:
Heavenly Father, thank You for taking great delight in me and rejoicing over me with singing. I pray that I would have an accurate perspective of Who You truly are and the way You see me. I want to be captivated by You and make You the utmost delight

and pleasure of my life. I choose to do life with You, every moment of every day. Lead me in all ways. In Jesus' name, amen.

Seek

"But seek first the kingdom of God and His righteousness, and all these things shall be added to you." - Matthew 6:33

When we seek Him first, God says He will add "all things" to our lives. This promise is preceded by verses reminding us not to worry about our lives and where our provision will come from. He clothes the lilies of the valleys and feeds the birds of the air, and He assures us, the ones He carefully crafted and made in His likeness, of provision as well.

He is the ultimate source of everything we need in life. When we are tempted to let our trust in Him wane, we can remind ourselves of His Word, stand on His truth, and choose to refocus our attention on seeking Him. Our part is to seek Him; His part is to take care of us.

What does it mean to seek His Kingdom, and how do we do it? Romans 14:17 tells us that the Kingdom of God is "righteousness, peace, and joy." Pursuing those things that are Kingdom-focused looks like reading, knowing and adhering to His Word, spending time in His presence, and being obedient to the call of God on our life as we walk in relationship with Him.

Matthew 7:8 tells us that "he who seeks finds." When we are seeking God wholeheartedly, He will be found (Jeremiah 29:13). He wants us to seek His face and to know Him well. God is not playing hide and seek with humanity; we don't have to look hard to find Him. I imagine us searching for Him all the while He is standing in plain sight waving His arms in the air, saying, "here I am!".

Not only does He want us to find Him, He passionately pursues us as well. "What do you think? If a man owns a hundred sheep, and one of them wanders away, will he not leave the ninety-nine on the hills and go to look for the one that wandered off?" (Matthew 16:13). Jesus is the Good Shepherd (John 10:11). He does not let His sheep (people) wander aimlessly without attempting to bring them into a place of safety (relationship with Him).

When our minds are plagued with endless questions, doubt, and worry, our simple solution is to call on Him for the answers. Jeremiah 33:3 says that when we do, He will answer us. When we find Him, we find everything - our life's purpose, answers to our questions, meaning, value, truth. All that we need is found in Him, the One worth seeking Who is always seeking us.

Ponder verses: Psalm 27:4; 1 Chronicles 16:11; 2 Peter 1:3; James 1:17

Prayer:

Heavenly Father, thank You for finding me when I was wandering aimlessly through life. I know that You are not hiding Yourself from me and that when I call upon You, You promise to answer. I turn away from all doubt, worry and fear and choose to look to You instead. I will seek first Your Kingdom and trust You to provide for everything that I need in life. In Jesus' name, amen.

Shine Brightly

"You are the light of the world. A city that is set on a hill cannot be hidden." - Matthew 5:14

You were not created to hide the light that is in you. Hiding is often indicative of shame, embarrassment, and insecurity, all of which have no place in the heart and life of a believer. Romans 1:16 is a statement we should readily adopt as our own mindset: *I am not ashamed of the gospel of Christ*. The gospel is the good news of the life, death, and resurrection of Jesus Christ; news that when received, accepted, and applied to our lives, has the power to transform and change us.

The light that you carry is the light of Christ and is exactly what our grappling, lost culture needs. Our world is plagued by ever-increasing darkness *(For behold, the darkness shall cover the earth, and deep darkness the people; but the LORD will arise over you, and His glory will be seen upon you. - Isaiah 60:2)*. The only way to eradicate darkness is to flood it with light.

Why shine? We find that answer in Matthew 5:16: *let your light shine before others so that they may see your good works and give glory to your Father who is in heaven*. When we shine, it brings glory to God. I heard a quote once that says, "don't shine to be seen. Shine so that, through you, others may see Him." The reason we shine is so that others can encounter a God who deeply loves them and wants to do life with them.

We can't wait for people to meet God at a church service or through our pastor; we are all commissioned to be ministers of reconciliation (2 Corinthians 5:20), and that most often happens outside of a church building. By examining the life of Jesus, we can see that most of His ministry did not happen at the religious buildings. He met people where they were - in the streets, in homes, at their workplaces, and even at a graveyard. There is no place off-limits to Him.

When you carry the light of God within you, you become a lighthouse for others. The ways that you emit light are through your words and actions; the things you say and the way you live your life either shines or hides the light. We are called to shift atmospheres, not adapt and conform to them. This means that anywhere you go - work, the gas station, or church - you are called to display His light to those around you. As you boldly project God's light, you will guide others to the safest harbor that exists - a relationship with Him. So shine His light brightly!

Ponder verses: John 8:12; Ephesians 5:8; 2 Corinthians 4:6; 1 Peter 2:9

Prayer:
Heavenly Father, thank You for creating me to be a light to the world. I pray that I shine Your light brightly and represent You well in all that I do. I ask for boldness to share Your love and

truth unashamedly. I want to be a lighthouse for others, pointing them to You. Thank You for grace and mercy for the times I haven't represented You well and the chance to start now. In Jesus' name, amen.

First Love Intimacy

"love the Lord your God with all your heart, with all your soul, with all your mind, and with all your strength" - Mark 12:30

Loving God more than anything sounds absurd until you experience the way that He loves You. When you do, you can't help but love Him back with an unrelenting, fervent, abandoned kind of love; a love that puts nothing and no one above Him. This is the place of intimacy He is calling all of us to, a place that puts Him in the highest place of priority and position in our lives.

A love that holds nothing back is the kind of love God requires of us. Romans 5:8 tells us that Jesus demonstrated His love for us at the cross. He didn't wait for us to "get our act together" or even love Him first before He chose to love us the way He does. It was love that sent Him to earth to begin with (see John 3:16), and it is love that motivates Him to continually pursue us throughout the entirety of our lives.

Maintaining the fervent love we feel towards God when we first become followers is a must. That does not mean we have to be at the pinnacle of a proverbial mountaintop at every moment of our existence; that's unrealistic. It does, however, mean that regardless of what we endure in this life, we do not abandon our relationship with Him. In the high moments, we love Him, and in the low moments, we love Him. The way we love Him is unchanged and unphased by the circumstances of our lives.

In the book of Revelation, we read about a church in Ephesus that is commended by God for their incredible works. They were doing mighty things for the cause of Christ, yet in the process of "doing," they abandoned their first love intimacy. In His kindness, He calls them to a place of repentance. He beckons them back to the place where they first fell in love with Him. This is the same call to us as believers today; to not live our lives in a place of service *for* Him at the expense of forsaking our first love intimacy *with* Him.

How do we get that first love back? In Revelation 2:5, the Ephesians church is instructed to "do the first works." Think of the things you did with God when you first fell in love with Him. The time you spent in His Word and in His presence. The way you shared His love without hesitation. The joy you felt with your newfound freedom in Him. He is beckoning you back to a place of first love intimacy where you love Him more than anyone and anything else.

Ponder verses: John 3:16; Romans 2:4; Revelation 2:2-5

Prayer:

Heavenly Father, thank You for drawing me back to a place of first love intimacy with You. I want to love You with every fiber of my being and to put nothing before You. Let all that I do be from a place of intimacy with You. Your love is worth my entire existence. In Jesus' name, amen.

First Love Poem

Shake us from our slumber, disturb the apathy
Awake us from our sleeping, break all complacency

Fill us with unquenching zeal and blazing passion for Your name
Let us experience You in such a way we'll never be the same

Interrupt our own agendas; we lay down our man-made plans
We want to hear from Heaven, to seek Your face, not just Your hand

We declare a return to our first love, a longing to know You more
We want to love You deeper than we ever have before

Boil the lukewarm waters, so we're hot for You again
Ignite a burning spark inside us, fan the flame within

Keeping oil in our lamps, we will not be lulled to sleep
We silence enemy lies and serve him total vacancy

To know You and to make You known is the deepest desire of our heart
We trust fully in Your faithfulness to finish what You start

Let us see a lost and broken world both healed and returned
By the power of the gospel and the truth of Your Word

Radiant

"Those who look to Him are radiant; their faces are never covered with shame." - Psalm 34:5 NIV

To look means to *"direct one's gaze toward someone or something or in a specified direction."*

When we look to God, our countenance changes. He transforms our appearance from gloom to glory, downtrodden to delighted, perplexed to peaceful, razzled to radiant. You can't look to and spend time with the God of all creation and not experience a perceptible difference. Keeping our gaze latched heavenward is pivotal to navigating life with all of its ups and downs.

Stephen's story of unabated faith is shared in Acts 6 and 7. He was a man of good reputation, described as full of faith, power, wisdom, and the Holy Spirit. He did great wonders and signs, answering an expressed need within his community to minister to widows. His boldness and demonstration of the Spirit's power attracted religious opposition, ultimately resulting in his martyrdom by stoning.

In the final scene of his life, as he stood boldly before a group of falsely accusing religious leaders, he chose to shift his focus from the heated confrontation to Heaven. In the most pressure-filled moment of his life, He looked up and "saw the glory of God, and Jesus standing at the right hand of God" (Acts 7:55). As he was hastily escorted out of the city to be stoned to death, he exhibited grace, mercy, and forgiveness toward those who murdered him.

Even in the moments when the world would have justified his retaliation, he chose the way of love and never veered from the narrow path. How do we stay unwavering in our faith like Stephen did? I believe the key to Stephen's persistence in the trial and ability to endure hardship without wavering was that his eyes were already looking heavenward before the time of pressure came. He was already fully persuaded of God's truth and convinced of his convictions, making the circumstances around him powerless to sway him.

There are moments in life when looking to God feels effortless, and other times when maintaining our vantage is more laborious and muddied. Staying steadfast in our relationship with God, keeping our eyes continually fixed on Him in the good times and the bad, is essential for longevity in our faith journey. Resolve firmly to fix your gaze on our glorious God, the One who reflects His radiance upon your face and never covers you with shame.

Ponder verses: Isaiah 50:7; Isaiah 61:7; 2 Corinthians 4:6

Prayer:

Heavenly Father, thank You for the ability to have a heavenward perspective. I desire to keep my eyes locked with You in every season of my life, whether good or bad. I know that You promise to work all things together for my good according to Romans 8:28. I want people to see Your radiance upon my face; let them see You in me, Lord. In Jesus' name, amen.

Behold

"One thing I have desired of the Lord, that will I seek: that I may dwell in the house of the Lord all the days of my life, to behold the beauty of the Lord, and to inquire in His temple" - Psalm 27:4

The ability to dwell, behold and inquire of the Lord were all what David penned in Psalms as his primary privileges and deepest desires. In a time when the Holy Spirit had not yet been placed within God's people, David longed to be in the house of the Lord because that was where His presence dwelt. He didn't seek these things sporadically; he desired them daily.

Beholding God's beauty was an act of worship that a woman named Mary demonstrated well. In Luke 10, we read about Jesus visiting the home of a woman named Martha. While she was distracted with serving her guests, her sister Mary sat at Jesus' feet and listened. Understandably, her lack of help serving frustrated Martha. When she vented her annoyances to the Lord, He not only defended Mary, He also affirmed that her action of sitting at His feet and listening was better than all of the hustle and bustle that Martha was doing.

We are all like Martha in many ways. We get so distracted by "doing" for God that we neglect and forget to just be with Him - sitting in His presence and listening like Mary did. We habitually ask God to bless our perfectly laid out plans and fail to inquire of His will and ask for His input in the matter. We buy into busyness and bypass the precious privilege of seeking Him, a desire David longingly expressed. We take for granted the ability we have to simply be with Him.

God wants to communicate with us. As temples of God, we carry His Holy Spirit's presence within us. New Covenant believers have the awesome privilege of hearing His voice (John 10:27) and inquiring of Him (James 1:5). The Holy Spirit will lead you into all truth and show you of things to come (John 16:13). He will remind you of who He is and who you are in Him. He will do all of these things and so much more as you simply set aside the time to spend with Him.

Don't take for granted the access you have been given to the God of the universe and the reality that He *wants* to spend time with you. You are not an inconvenience or a disruption to Him. There will come a day when we will all stand before Him face to face, but we don't have to wait until we take our last breath to meet with Him. While we exist on this side of eternity, let's choose to do "the better thing" like Mary did, sitting at His feet, listening and beholding Him.

Ponder verses: Acts 7:48; Acts 17:24; 1 Corinthians 13:12; Hebrews 10:19-20

Prayer:

Heavenly Father, thank You for placing Your Holy Spirit within me. I pray that I would not be so distracted by busyness that I forget the awesome privilege I have of spending time with You. God, I want a desire like David did to daily dwell with, behold and inquire of You. There is nothing better or more important to me. In Jesus' name, amen.

Inescapable

"Where can I go from Your Spirit? Or where can I flee from Your presence? If I ascend into heaven, You are there; if I make my bed in hell, behold, You are there." - Psalm 139:7-8

Our Maker is in constant pursuit of us, and there is nowhere we can go to flee from His presence. His Spirit is never off-limits; He meets us exactly where we are. We have to get out of the mindset that He only dwells within the four walls of a church. Yes, He can be found in a church building, but He can also be found in a jail cell, a hospital bed, a bar, and even the bread aisle of the grocery store. He is omnipresent, meaning He is present everywhere.

There is not one place that He won't go to meet with us, to reveal Himself and to prove His love.

The life and ministry of Jesus on the earth persuades us of the deep love God has for people and the truth that He isn't waiting for us to come to Him; He is chasing after us.

Jesus always welcomed in and sought out the outcasts of society. Those that the world called disposable, He considered worthy of pursuit. He encountered and healed many lepers, diseased outcasts deemed as untouchable by society. One account in Matthew 8 describes a man that came and knelt before Jesus, asking to be cleansed. Jesus not only healed him, but He touched him before He did so, a taboo and forbidden action that perfectly demonstrated a God whose love is not restricted. In Luke 17, we read about a band of unclean lepers, ten to be exact. Jesus grants all of them healing, but only one returns to give thanks and glory to God. Jesus knew that they wouldn't all come back, yet He did not withhold healing from them.

He does the same for us today. James 1:17 tells us that "every good and perfect gift" comes from Him. He pours out His goodness and blessings to those He knows will never give Him credit. He doesn't give of Himself because of our own merit or what He can receive in return; He does it because it's who He is - good.

He freely gives His love to humanity with no regard for reciprocation. Even at the most excruciatingly painful point of His life as He hung naked, bloodied, and beaten on a cross, He still lovingly looked down at those who put Him there and uttered words of forgiveness. He will never stop pursuing you, no matter where you find yourself in life. His love is inescapable.

Ponder verses: Psalm 23:6; Psalm 139; Psalm 145:9

Prayer:
Heavenly Father, thank You for loving me so much. I know that there isn't a place I can go and not find Your Spirit and Your presence - You are everywhere. I am so thankful that you are always with me, that You go before me and behind me, that You

surround me, and You're within me. I pray that I would pursue people and showcase Your love to the world. I pray that I would never see anyone as unreachable or untouchable, only as loved and redeemable. Let me love others the way that You do. In Jesus' name, amen.

Faithful Love

"For the Lord is good and His love endures forever; His faithfulness continues through all generations." - Psalm 100:5 NIV

God isn't waiting for us to check all of the right boxes and jump through fictitious hoops to show His faithfulness. The reality is there is nothing we can do to change the steadfastness of His character. Hebrews 6:18 describes God as "immutable." This means that He is unable to be changed. 2 Timothy 2:13 tells us that "if we are faithless, He remains faithful; He cannot deny Himself." Faithfulness is a fixed attribute of who He is that is independent of anything we do. He remains loyal regardless of our reciprocation.

Often when we first fall in love, we display our affections without a second thought. We do things with and for the one we love with no regard to the sacrifice it takes. Over time, love can become something we start attaching stipulations to and we moderate giving it away so freely. This can also easily happen in the way we receive and respond to God's love and the salvation He has given us. Initially, we know and understand that His love and salvation is a free gift of grace with no works attached (Ephesians 2:8), but then we somehow convince ourselves that we have to do things in order to keep it.

God is faithful to keep His covenant of love towards you regardless of what you do or don't do. The Bible reminds us that nothing in all of creation can separate us from His love (Romans 8:38). He loved us before we even *could* love Him, and He isn't rescinding His love for any reason. When we abide in relationship with Him, good works will naturally overflow from a place of intimacy; they will never be what puts us in right standing with Him or a means to earn His love. The only string attached to His love is our willingness to receive it.

He is not only faithful to love us, He is also faithful to keep His word and fulfill His promises. He cannot lie (Hebrews 6:18), so we can stand on the truth of scripture and what His Spirit speaks to us, knowing that He will always do what He says He will do. Reading His Word reveals His promises for all people. Spending time in His presence, seeking His face, and listening acutely to His voice reveals His promises for us individually. Being open to hearing Him speak gives us vitality, strengthens our hope, and increases our faith in the One who will never change and will always remain forever faithful.

Ponder verses: Deuteronomy 7:9; Psalm 33:4; Hebrews 10:23; Hebrews 13:8

Prayer:
Heavenly Father, thank You for Your constant faithfulness. I choose to stand on the truth of Your Word and the things You have spoken to me regardless of what things look like. I know that You will keep every promise You make and fulfill every part of Your plan for my life. I willingly say "yes" to Your faithful love. Use my life to display Your unchanging love and faithfulness to those around me. In Jesus' name, amen.

Vast

"Your love, Lord, reaches to the heavens, Your faithfulness to the skies." - Psalm 36:5 NIV

It's impossible to fully grasp or understand the vast and immeasurable way that God loves us. Ephesians 3:16-18 is a prayer penned by the Apostle Paul that describes God's love as wide, high, long, and deep. Every form of existing measurement is listed, and still unable to perfectly articulate the vastness of His magnificent love. It's a love that is unfailing, unchanging, and unrelenting, and greater than any other love that we could ever experience.

The capacity of God to love each of us in such a distinguished, personal way is beyond our ability to fully comprehend. The very One who breathed stars into existence (Psalm 33:6) and knows each one by name (Psalm 147:4) also personally knows and desires intimacy with us. He wants more than a casual, infrequent relationship; He wants all that we are, even if we feel like what we have to offer Him is fragmented. God is not intimidated by our brokenness. He fully perceives our frailty and loves us enough to undo the damage. He is not waiting for us to piece ourselves together first; outside of Him, true healing and wholeness isn't even possible anyway.

Some of the many redeeming actions Jesus came to execute are found in Isaiah 61:1 - healing for the brokenhearted, freedom for the captives, and release for prisoners from darkness. Anything that we have, or ever will endure and experience that has resulted in brokenness, captivity, or darkness is redeemable by God's only begotten Son, Jesus. When we invite Him into our brokenness, He invites us into wholeness. Compassion is then spurred in us for others still bound in the brokenness we have broken out of. The beauty of a story redeemed by God is that it carries the power and effectiveness to set others free in the same ways we have experienced. When we stand in victory on the other side of defeat, we can be a voice to those still stuck in oppression and show them the way to freedom.

"Forget the former things; do not dwell on the past. See, I am doing a new thing!" (Isaiah 43: 18). He is a God who makes all things new, and there is an urgency to release things in our past so that we can move forward into the new things He has for us. Seasons are not meant to last forever, and we must refuse the urge to resist letting Him move and manifest in new ways. We are being called to new seasons, new depths, and new levels of intimacy, and in those deep and intimate places, we will discover more of His immeasurable, vast love for us.

Ponder verses: Song of Solomon 5:1; Ephesians 3:16-18; 1 John 3:1

Prayer:

Heavenly Father, thank You for loving me in such an immeasurable way and for not allowing me to stay stuck in any form of bondage or brokenness. I give You permission to heal anything in my life that is broken. I acknowledge You as my Healer and the only One who can truly set me free. Help me to use my story so that others can know Your same rescuing love and power. In Jesus' name, amen.

Ask Seek Knock

"Ask, and it will be given to you; seek and you will find; knock, and the door will be opened to you."
- Matthew 7:7

Persistency has the power to persuade even the most unrelenting person. In scripture, God permits us to pray persistently. Tenacity in prayer is a concept that many are too timid to exhibit but is the exact ingredient we need to change our prayers from impotent to powerful. In James 5:16, the fervent prayer of a righteous person (someone in right standing with God) is described as powerful and effective, able to accomplish much. Fervency indicates passion and intensity. Praying should never be viewed as boring, lifeless, and dull, but as vibrant, heartfelt, and enthusiastic; after all, prayer is engaging with the Almighty God Himself.

We can enter His throne room with boldness (Hebrews 4:16), so approaching God should never be done in a mouse-like manner. He wants His children to know that they have access to Him and can approach Him as such. 1 John 5:14 reminds us that we can have confidence and know that when we pray according to His will, He hears us. Knowing His will can be found within His Word and His presence.

In scripture, we read of two parables (stories) Jesus told that paint a picture of persistence in prayer. Luke 18 tells the tale of a persistent widow to show us how we "always ought to pray and not lose heart" (verse 1). She exhibited faith by her persistence in going before an unjust judge to seek justice against her adversary. His reluctance to respond turned to persuasion because of her perseverance and unwillingness to back down from her request. In Luke 11, Jesus models prayer to His disciples ("the Lord's prayer"), then immediately tells a story about someone who came to the home of his friend at an inconvenient time (midnight) seeking bread for his household. Verse 8 tells us, "I say to you, though he will not rise and give to him because he is his friend, yet because of his persistence, he will rise and give him as many as he needs."

Persistence precedes breakthroughs in prayer. We are promised that when we ask, we will receive; when we seek, we will find; when we knock, the door will be opened. The problem is never God's unwillingness to answer our prayers; it's in our reluctance to actually pray. It's time for us to begin to ask, seek and knock like we never have before.

Ponder verses: Psalm 84:11; Isaiah 59:1; 2 Corinthians 9:8

Prayer:
Heavenly Father, thank You for the privilege I have to bring my requests before You. I want to pray according to Your will,

knowing that when I do, You hear me. Stir in me a desire to pray passionately and persistently. I know that my prayers have the power to move mountains, effect change, and shake up the world. Thank you for showing me how to pray and reminding me that my fervent prayers are both effective and accomplish much. In Jesus' name, amen.

Come Home

"He arose and came to his father. But when he was still a great way off, his father saw him and had compassion, and ran and fell on his neck and kissed him." - Luke 15:20

Compassion is one of the many beautiful attributes of our Heavenly Father displayed in the parable of the lost son (Luke 15). In this parable, a son takes his inheritance early, leaves home, and squanders it on wayward living. At the lowest point in his journey, the Bible says, "he came to himself." His eyes were opened to the reality of his poor decisions and what he gave up by leaving his father's house, and he decided to return home.

As he meekly approached home, his father's greeting was not at all what he had expected. He was not met with condemnation, scolding, and "I told you so"; he was met with mercy, love, and compassion. He was clothed with his father's best robe, a ring on his hand, and sandals for his feet, and his father threw a party in celebration of his return.

How often do we expect God to meet us with shame when we mess up and come back to Him? We instinctively anticipate a finger-wagging session, yet that is not at all how He deals with us. He rejoices when we come to Him and reminds us of our inheritance.

The robe He covers us with is one of righteousness (Isaiah 61:10). The ring He places on our finger is one of covenant and authority (Luke 10:19). The shoes He puts on our feet are peace-filled (Ephesians 6:15), displaying that we are not subservient, but sons of God (Galatians 4:7).

The great commission (instruction, command, duty) Jesus gave His followers before He ascended to Heaven was to "make disciples of all nations." This is a clarion call to invite others into a relationship with Him. It is vital that we, as believers, pray for "prodigal" loved ones (those who don't know God). The Word says in 2 Corinthians 4:4 that "the god of this age has blinded (people) who do not believe." Pray for nonbelievers to have their eyes opened to the truth of God's love for them. 2 Peter 3:9 articulates His desire for none to perish and for everyone to come to a place of repentance (turning their lives toward Him).

Our message to the world must never be one of shame or condemnation because that is an inaccurate display of God's character. We meet people the way He did, with compassion, mercy, and love. The message is never "where have you been"; it's always "just come home."

Ponder verses: Psalm 103:2; Matthew 28:19-20

Prayer:
Heavenly Father, thank You for welcoming me home with open arms and giving me Your best robe, ring, and sandals. I ask You

to seat the truth of Your great love and compassion deep within my heart. I pray for anyone who does not know You to come into a relationship with You. I want them to experience the fullness of Your love and mercy. I know that this world has nothing for me, and with You is where I truly long to be. In Jesus' name, amen.

Silence

"There is a time for everything, and a season for every activity under the heavens...a time to be silent and a time to speak" - *Ecclesiastes 3:1 & 7b*

As the busyness of life swirls around us, we must intentionally choose to remove our gaze from other things and lock eyes with Him. Stillness is an act of discipline that dismisses distraction and invites His presence to overwhelm and change us. It's a place where we can settle our hearts before the Creator of the universe and fix our focus on nothing else but Him.

The gaze of His fiery, love-filled eyes removes shame, insecurity, doubt, anxiety, fear, depression, sadness, loneliness and replaces anything not of and from Him with pure truth. We can never find our validation in other people's opinions or the standards our corrupt world creates. Only in Him can we find unerring purpose, identity, and security.

Often when God does speak, it isn't in a loud and extremely obvious manner (see 1 Kings 19). It's often in a still, small voice that we could easily mistake as our own thoughts. As His sheep (followers), we have the privilege of hearing His voice and the opportunity to obey. We can practice hearing His voice by quieting ourselves and simply asking Him to speak to us. One-way communication, where we are the only ones saying anything, is a form of prayer that many fall into, not realizing that God also has things He wants to speak to us.

In moments when He seems silent, it may just be a divine invitation to press in and simply bask in His presence, to spend time seeking and beholding His face without the need to receive anything more than just the privilege of being with Him. When we feel like we don't understand what God is saying and doing, we can rest in His faithfulness and on the solid foundation of His unchanging written Word.

Like Ecclesiastes says, there are times in our lives for both speaking and silence. That truth applies to both us and to God. In the silent seasons of life, stay encouraged, knowing that God is always faithful (2 Timothy 2:13), He is always for you (Romans 8:31), and He is always working things together for your good (Romans 8:28). Remember that His thoughts for you are innumerable (Psalm 139:18) and that Jesus is interceding in Heaven on your behalf (Romans 8:34). His unchanging character, His everlasting love, and His unfailing Word reminds our hearts that He has not forgotten us, even in seasons of silence.

Ponder verses: Matthew 6:8; John 10:14; John 10:27; 2 Timothy 2:19

Prayer:

Heavenly Father, thank You for the divine invitation of being with You and spending time in Your presence. I never want the distractions of this world to take away from my intimate time with You. I invite You into every area of my life and ask You to remove anything that is not of You and replace it with what is. I trust You, and I love you. In Jesus' name, amen.

Searched

"O LORD, You have searched me and known me." - Psalm 139:1

There is something so profoundly beautiful about being fully known by a God Whose love never wavers or changes despite our failures, flaws, and mistakes. We serve a Savior Who didn't wait for us to find Him but instead searched us out. He is the One who initiated a relationship with us; our ability to know Him was His idea and a result of His great love. We did nothing to deserve it, and all we have to do is accept and receive it.

Jesus spoke and taught in ways that those who had ears to hear (in other words, whose spiritual ears were open to receive the messages He spoke) could relate to as far as cultural context is concerned. Matthew 18:12 tells the parable of the lost sheep:

What do you think? If a man owns a hundred sheep, and one of them wanders away, will he not leave the ninety-nine on the hills and go to look for the one that wandered off? And if he finds it, truly I tell you, he is happier about that one sheep than about the ninety-nine that did not wander off.

The Bible tells us that when one sinner repents, Heaven has a party (Luke 15:7 and 10). We serve a God who eagerly pursues those who are wandering and restores lives to wholeness in Him. He understands that this world has a way of pulling and luring us into traps that are not His best for us. He doesn't just leave us in those traps, hoping we will find a way of escape and then come to Him; He finds us in those traps and rescues us from them.

There is no sin too wicked, dark, or dirty that would keep Him from pursuing and wanting you. He does not ostracize anyone. 2 Peter 3:9 tells us that "He is not willing that any should perish." His heart is for everyone to know Him. Luke 19:10 tells us the express purpose Jesus came to earth to begin with: "to seek and save that which was lost." Mark 2:17 reiterates the mission of Jesus: "Those who are well have no need of a physician, but those who are sick. I did not come to call the righteous, but sinners, to repentance."

Jesus came to give us a way out of the entanglements of sin and to show us the path of freedom in Him. This world has many lures and traps to keep us from God's best, but we can choose to forsake the wandering and let Him lead our lives. He will never stop searching for those who are lost. He is in a passionate, unrelenting pursuit of His creation - you!

Ponder verses: 2 Peter 3:9; Luke 19:10; Mark 2:17

Prayer:
Heavenly Father, thank You for leaving the ninety-nine to find me. I choose today to walk in the freedom You have for me, leaving my past behind and pressing on in my faith race in obedient

surrender. I pray for those who don't know You to be found by You. In Jesus' name, amen.

Holy

"Pursue peace with all people, and holiness, without which no one will see the Lord" - Hebrews 12:14

We are called to a life of holiness and purity, which can only be done through the work of the Holy Spirit. The Bible says that no good thing dwells in our flesh (Romans 7:18); that is our human nature separate from Him. A life of holiness is not a life of perfection; it's a life set apart unto Him. We are called to reflect Him and to be holy because He is holy (1 Peter 1:16).

Jesus called the pure in heart blessed (Matthew 5:8), and the privilege of purity is to see God. One of the descriptions of pure religion is to keep ourselves from being polluted by the world (James 1:27). God's standards supersede what culture defines as acceptable. We live in a world that is increasingly growing corrupt and consistently moving further from the truth of God's Word. In a culture that attempts to redefine right and wrong, we must stand firmly on the foundation of God's Word, refusing to be swayed by anything that goes against our fixed point of reference (the Bible). Jesus tells us that if we love Him, we will obey His commandments (John 14:15) and that His commandments are not burdensome (1 John 5:3). It is a joy to follow His ways, even when it goes against the grain.

The most intimate form of earthly love is marriage. Repeatedly in scripture, the church (God's people) is described as the bride of Christ. As His bride, we are called to consecration and to prepare ourselves for His return. I want to remind your heart that He is coming back.

Let us rejoice and be glad and give him glory! For the wedding of the Lamb has come, and his bride has made herself ready. Fine linen, bright and clean, was given her to wear." (Fine linen stands for the righteous acts of God's holy people.) Then the angel said to me, "Write this: Blessed are those who are invited to the wedding supper of the Lamb!" And he added, "These are the true words of God." (Revelation 19:7-9)

God has invited all of us to a relationship with Him, yet the sad reality is that some will decline His invitation. The standard He calls us to is a sacrifice some will never willingly surrender to. In His goodness, we are given free will and the choice to choose Him. When we do say "yes" to Him, He walks us through the journey of becoming more like Him (Romans 8:29). He has called us, as His bride, to be without spot or wrinkle, to be holy and blameless (Ephesians 5:27). Are you ready for His return, and will you say "yes" to His invitation of holiness?

Ponder verses: Isaiah 5:20; Luke 14:16-24; Ephesians 2:10;

Prayer:
Heavenly Father, thank You for the ability to be holy and set apart unto You. I want my life to reflect the beauty of my relationship with You. Purify me in every way and make me more like You. I say "yes" to all that You have for me and all that You call me to. In Jesus' name, amen.

Breakthrough

"Let us not become weary in doing good, for at the proper time we will reap a harvest if we do not give up." - Galatians 6:9 NIV

Breakthrough happens when we refuse to give up before we see the manifestation of what we are believing God for. What moves your heart matters. Pay attention to the passions God has put within you. Often, we don't realize that the very things that fire us up are the things we are called to pray for and do something about. Is there a certain injustice, cause, or happening in the world that riles you?

God is calling His people to be watchmen. 1 Timothy 6:20 says, "Guard what was committed to your trust." We have all been given precious things to guard and protect - our own lives, families, communities, and ministries. Whatever God has placed in our world, we are called to tend, and He has given us everything we need to do so. As we stand confidently, calling things that are not as though they are (Romans 4:17) and seeing the future through the eyes of faith, we will be able to pray effectively. When we intercede through prayer for people, places, and situations, which simply means to intervene on behalf, we refuse to sit on the sidelines and do nothing; we are taking action and allowing God to use us to make a difference.

So often, we are programmed to be reactionary in prayer. We live with our guard down, allowing the enemy to wreak havoc on our lives. After he makes a mess, we attempt to clean up the aftermath of his destruction. I believe God is calling His people to move from a defensive stance to a mode of offense, to allow the Holy Spirit to reveal things to come (John 16:13), and to dismantle the enemy's plans before they play out. You, believer, have the resurrection power of Jesus Christ living inside of you, and because of that, you can and will do the works Jesus did and greater (John 14:12). You were not made for a mediocre existence; you were created to bring breakthroughs to every sphere of influence God has given you.

We are called to walk by faith, not by sight. What we see with our spiritual eyes must supersede what we see with our natural eyes. Scripture tells us that mustard seed faith has the ability to move mountains. Mustard seeds are known for their strength and tenacity. Our faith becomes tenacious when we allow it to grow, and it grows by the Word of God. As we read, believe, and apply the Word of God to our lives, our faith will increase. Let's choose to stand boldly in faith until we see the breakthrough we believe Him for.

Ponder verses: Isaiah 52:8; Matthew 17:20; Romans 10:17; 2 Corinthians 5:7; Hebrews 11:6

Prayer:

Heavenly Father, thank You for Your Word and Your promises. I choose today to stand in Your strength and believe for breakthrough. I pray against weariness and anything that is coming against me, tempting me to give up. I ask for wisdom and revelation as I read Your Word and grow in my faith. I want to live a life that glorifies You. In Jesus' name, amen.

Sow in Tears

"Those who sow in tears shall reap in joy." - Psalm 126:5

Life is hard. This is not a revelation for any of us; it's a fact. Jesus told His followers that in this world, we would have many troubles, but to take heart because He overcame the world (John 16:33). While life may not always be all we hope for, we can have peace knowing that we never walk through anything alone.

Our cries never fall on deaf ears. The Bible promises in Psalm 34:17 that "the righteous cry out and the Lord hears." We can be confident that when we go through the trials and tribulations of life and call out to God, He is right there waiting and willing to move on our behalf.

Desperation will drive people to call out to God in a way they maybe otherwise wouldn't. In Luke chapter 18, we read about a blind man who sat by the road begging. Most likely, this was the way he spent most of his time, but this particular day was one that would change the course of the rest of his life. He heard the commotion of the crowd around him and asked what was going on. When they let him know that Jesus was passing by, he cried out, saying, "Jesus, Son of David, have mercy on me!" (Luke 18:38). Everyone around him told him to be quiet, but their insistence was met with his persistence as he chose to vacate their requests and cried out "all the more." His cries captured the attention of Jesus, Who answered this beggar's request to receive his sight. He began following Jesus and glorifying God, and those people around him who were just moments prior telling him to be quiet began giving praise to God.

When we find ourselves in desperate circumstances where we truly need a touch from God Almighty, we cannot let the voices of others drown out what He has spoken to our hearts. We must resolve, like the beggar, to only get louder with our cries until we receive an answer.

There is a promise of joy after a night of pain and weeping (Psalm 30:5). Some seasons feel like they are drowned by pools of tears as the aches of our sometimes broken lives produce pain beyond our ability to bear. In those seasons of seemingly never-ending disappointments, failures, and frustrations, we must train ourselves to turn to the One whose yoke is easy and whose burden is light. Our cries are heard by the God of all creation (Psalm 34:15), and our tears are sowing seeds that will one day reap a harvest of joy.

Ponder verses: Psalm 6:8-9; Psalm 57:2; Psalm 145:19; Matthew 11:28-30

Prayer:

Heavenly Father, thank You for hearing my cries. I am so grateful that You are attentive to me and that You care about everything that moves my heart and matters to me. God, I ask You to show me how to pray for my family, community, church, ministries, and the world around me. I want to pray for people, places, and situations with faith and confidence that You will move in all of it, and change will come. Have Your way, God. In Jesus' name, amen.

Access

"Therefore He is also able to save to the uttermost those who come to God through Him since He always lives to make intercession for them."
- Hebrews 7:25

Prior to Jesus' death on the cross, God's presence dwelt in the Temple within a place called the Holy of Holies. A very thick veil was in place to separate the presence of God from the outside world. When Jesus breathed His last breath on the cross, the veil in the temple was torn in two. God's presence is no longer confined to a room within the Temple; His presence now dwells within every born-again believer (1 Corinthians 3:16).

We must always remember that we are seated with Christ in Heavenly places (Ephesians 2:6). This temporal world is not our home, and the access we have to God is available to us on this side of eternity. We are privileged to come before the throne of God with boldness (Hebrews 4:16). This means that we don't have to be shy, timid, or apprehensive to approach God; we can confidently go to Him in prayer and know He is ready and willing to interact with us.

Let this truth sink into your heart-you have the attention of the Creator of all things (Colossians 1:16). He is captivated by your very existence and loves you more than you can even comprehend. Jesus, the express image of God (Hebrews 1:3), displayed a love that let people in. As He walked the earth, Jesus gave the religious and the non-religious alike access to Himself. In every encounter, people were met with mercy, healing, forgiveness, and a proper perspective of the love of God. Some rejected Him completely, but those who didn't were changed forever.

Jesus' followers were a motley crew of misfits. His original twelve disciples came from all walks of life. God did not limit His followers to those of certain socio-economic status; His arms were, and still are, open to all willing to surrender everything to follow Him. Jesus bridged the gap between God and humanity, giving us unrestricted access to our Heavenly Father.

Access to God is not just reserved for pastors and church leaders; it's available to anyone. Access to God is not just reserved for Sunday mornings or special occasions; it's available any time day and night. Access to God is not just reserved for particular purposes; it's available to us during the significant and seemingly trivial moments of life. God wants us to know that we can experience Him at any time and in any place.

Ponder verses: Psalm 141:2; Matthew 27:51; Luke 23:45; Romans 8:34; 1 Timothy 1:5;

Prayer:
Heavenly Father, thank You for continual access to You. I love that I can come directly to You without having to go through

anyone else. I am so thankful that Your Holy Spirit lives within me and that I can come to You at any moment with confidence. I want to experience an intimate relationship with You and to know You more every day. In Jesus' name, amen.

Kindness

"God's kindness is intended to lead you to repentance" - Romans 2:4 NKJV

Kindness is a fruit of the Spirit, and therefore indicative of the character of God. Kind is Who He is. Throughout scripture and history, we see God's great love on display towards undeserving humanity. His love draws us into a relationship with Him and causes us to repent from our sinful nature and walk in the newness of life God has designed for us.

Repentance is more than an emotional response to the realization of our own depravity; it's an about-face action of turning away from one thing and turning towards another. On our faith journey, that looks like abandoning the world and turning toward God and His ways. James 4:4 tells us, "Do you not know that friendship with the world is enmity with God? Whoever therefore wants to be a friend of the world makes himself an enemy of God." We cannot serve both the Kingdom of God and this world; it's impossible. We are either all in with one or all in with the other. Joshua 24:15 is a call to "choose whom we will serve"; it's a choice we all get to make.

One of the assuring aspects of God's nature is that He never calls us to do anything He hasn't equipped us and given us the power to do. 2 Peter 1:3 reminds us that "His divine power has given to us all things that pertain to life and godliness." Living for God and walking according to the Spirit is possible and something all believers should desire to do.

In John 13, we read about the account of what we call "The Last Supper." Jesus is just days away from His arrest and crucifixion, and rather than sitting back and relaxing, enjoying His last moments on this earth, we see Him taking on the role of a servant. He humbly kneels at the feet of each of His disciples, even Judas Iscariot (the one who betrayed Him), and washes their feet. This was proof of Matthew 20:28, which says, "The Son of Man did not come to be served, but to serve, and to give His life a ransom for many.".

The kind nature of God is beautifully displayed throughout the Bible. We read about a Samaritan woman who met the kindness of God through an unexpected conversation with Jesus. We read about a woman caught in the act of adultery whose accusers' actions were canceled because of the kindness of Jesus. We read about the blind, deaf, lame, poor, and even the dead whose lives were eternally changed because of His lovingkindness. His kindness is still leading us to repentance today, giving us the desire to turn towards Him in all ways.

Ponder verses: Romans 6:4; Romans 12:2; Galatians 5:16; Colossians 3:9-10;

Prayer:
Heavenly Father, thank You for Your lovingkindness and for giving me everything that I need to live this life for You. I ask You to show me any area of my life where I have given more of my love and attention to this world rather than to You. I choose this day to live every moment of every day for You. I want to serve others the way You did, Jesus. In Jesus' name, amen.

Thankfulness

"Enter into His gates with thanksgiving and into His courts with praise. Be thankful to Him, and bless His name." - Psalm 100:4

Many grapple with perceiving and understanding the will of God, but did you know that throughout scripture, God lays out His universal will for His people? So many scriptures identify how we are to live our lives and also the calling God has placed on each of us. In 1 Thessalonians chapter 5, we are told to "give thanks in all circumstances; for this is God's will for you in Christ Jesus.". Thankfulness is God's will for our lives!

In a world full of doom and gloom, we are constantly bombarded with reasons to be invoked with fear, hopelessness, and despair. Despite all that this world is swirling with, we are still called to have hearts of gratitude. This is possible when we choose to forsake our earthly vantage point and see things through spiritual lenses. God has given us the ability to rise above whatever chaos is consuming the world around us and to stay seated in our rightful place, which is with Him in heavenly places (Ephesians 2:6). This means that we can acknowledge what is going on in the world around us, but also live in a place of peace, joy, and abundance despite it. No matter what we face, we are called to give Him thanks in all circumstances because He is worthy of our praise, adoration, and thankfulness.

Cultivating a grateful heart is one key to breaking free from the bondage of this world. When we begin to thank God for all that He has done and the things we believe Him for concerning our future, it changes our frame of mind. We are able to abandon anxiety, worry, and stress and function with faith, hope, and expectation. God's plans are only ever good, and He wants us to actually expect that He has good things for our lives. In Matthew 7, Jesus confirms this truth by urging His followers to ask, seek and knock and to know that our Heavenly Father is not going to give us less than we ask for. He actually wants to provide us with good things.

James 1:17 tells us that "every good and perfect gift is from above." This means that every good thing in our lives can be traced back to the hand of God. He withholds no good thing from us (Psalm 84:11), and His plans for us are good (Jeremiah 29:11). What can you thank God for today? I encourage you to make a list and thank Him out loud for everything you can think of. Do this often so that your heart stays tender towards His goodness and be thankful for all He has done and will do in your life.

Ponder verses: 1 Chronicles 16:34; Matthew 7:7-12; Ephesians 5:20; Philippians 2:14

Prayer:

Heavenly Father, thank You for all that You've done in my life and for always showing Yourself faithful to me. I know and believe that You have good things in store for my future, and I thank You in advance for them. You give good things to Your people, and I know that Your plans for me are only ever good. Thank You for the abundant blessings in my life. In Jesus' name, amen.

Measure the Distance

"As far as the east is from the west, so far has He removed our transgressions from us." - Psalm 103:12

The love of God cannot be measured, and neither can the space He places between us and our sin. The distance between the east and the west is incomputable. 1 John 1:9 says, "If we confess our sins, He is faithful and just to forgive us our sins and to cleanse us from all unrighteousness.". The prerequisite for forgiveness is simple - confess it. When we do, we are met with mercy because God is rich in mercy (Ephesians 2:4), He delights in showing mercy (Micah 7:18), and His mercies are new every morning (Lamentations 3:22-23).

When we are born again, our lives become hidden in Him (Colossians 3:3). "Therefore, if anyone is in Christ, he is a new creation; old things have passed away; behold, all things have become new." (2 Corinthians 5:17). God is able to take everything from our past, our mistakes, our failures, our sins, and give us an entirely new slate. As we journey through our relationship with Him, He continues to give us grace and the ability to walk in freedom and the newness of life. His grace is not a license to live our lives recklessly, but instead, it empowers us to live our lives by His standards and free from sin entanglements.

Love keeps no record of wrongs (1 Corinthians 13:5). Since God is love, we can rest assured that He is not sitting in Heaven tallying up every time we do something wrong. When we ask for forgiveness, He freely gives it and literally forgets (Hebrews 8:12). We can be confident that anytime we feel shame, embarrassment, or guilt over something we have asked God to forgive, it is the voice of our accuser (Satan). In those moments, we must silence his already powerless voice and remind ourselves that we are forgiven and free.

Once we have tasted and seen the goodness of God, we become "ministers of reconciliation." 2 Corinthians 5:18-21: *"Now all things are of God, who has reconciled us to Himself through Jesus Christ, and has given us the ministry of reconciliation, that is, that God was in Christ reconciling the world to Himself, not imputing their trespasses to them, and has committed to us the word of reconciliation. Now then, we are ambassadors for Christ, as though God were pleading through us: we implore you on Christ's behalf, be reconciled to God. For He made Him who knew no sin to be sin for us, that we might become the righteousness of God in Him.".* We have a call to tell others there is a God Who loves them with wide-open arms. He is ready and willing to remove sin and transgression from our lives by a distance that cannot be measured.

Ponder verses: 2 Corinthians 5:19-21; Titus 2:11-14; Revelation 12:10

Prayer:
Heavenly Father, thank You for Your grace, mercy, and forgiveness. I am in awe that You not only forgive my sin, but You forget it. Lord, use me to reconcile people to You. I want to tell others about Your love and to see them know You in a personal way. In Jesus' name, amen.

Truth

"Jesus said to him, "I am the way, the truth, and the life." No one comes to the Father except through Me." - John 14:6

Jesus promised His followers that He would not only prepare a place in paradise (Heaven) for them but that He would also come again and bring them to where He is. Jesus revealed Himself as the way, truth, and life in response to His disciple Thomas' question, "how can we know the way?" He made it abundantly clear that He is the bridge between an eternal God and otherwise hopeless humanity.

Throughout the Old Testament, scripture points to a Messiah (Jesus) who would one day restore what was lost in the Garden of Eden. We can read, study and meditate on the validated accounts and Words of Jesus Himself in the gospel books of the New Testament - Matthew, Mark, Luke, and John. One of the greatest lies and deceptive teachings is that multiple paths lead to the same destination (also known as religious relativism or universalism). Jesus made it abundantly clear that He is the only way to the Father.

Psalm 119:60 says, "the entirety of Your Word is truth." When we know the truth, the truth sets us free (John 8:32). Jesus is the truth, and when we know Him, we find freedom. Psalms 91 calls His truth our shield and buckler. Truth protects, guards, secures, and defends.

Luke 4:18 recites words Jesus spoke in congruence and fulfillment of prophecy in Isaiah 61:1 - *"The Spirit of the Lord is upon Me because He has anointed Me to preach the gospel to the poor; He has sent Me to heal the brokenhearted, to proclaim liberty to the captives and recovery of sight to the blind, to set at liberty those who are oppressed."*. Jesus came for a purpose, and He fulfilled that purpose. All that He came for He is still doing in the lives of people today.

As believers, we are called to carry His truth into the world around us. We know that repeatedly in scripture, we are called to love others; in fact, it's the second greatest commandment (John 13:34). Love is defined in 1 Corinthians 13, and part of the description of love is that it "rejoices in the truth" (verse 16). We must always speak the truth in love (Ephesians 4:15) and encourage others with the truth that God is for them, not against them, and that He came in the flesh to give them beauty for ashes, joy for mourning, and a garment of praise for the spirit of heaviness. The world needs to know that there is such a thing as absolute truth, and His name is Jesus.

Ponder verses: Proverbs 3:3-4; John 1:14; John 5:24; Galatians 5:1; 2 Timothy 2:15

Prayer:

Heavenly Father, thank You for Your truth. I pray that I would wholly follow all of Your ways, that I would rightly divide the Word of truth, and that I would live a life of truth. I pray against any deception or teachings that are false. I want Your truth to be deeply rooted in my heart and mind and to only speak what is aligned with Your truth. In Jesus' name, amen.

Steadfast

"The steadfast love of the Lord never ceases"
- Lamentations 3:22

God is faithfully committed to His people. His character is constant, and His pursuit of our hearts is unremitting. We can stand confidently on the God-breathed and Holy Spirit-inspired scriptures, knowing that He will never lie (Titus 1:2). He never changes, and He never will. He is Who He says He is, and He will do what He says He will do in, through, and for us.

We are called to a life of steadfast character, faith, and pursuit of Him. He has invited us to leave the destructive broad path of the world and journey the narrow one that He has paved (Matthew 7:14). This unpopular path is simultaneously full of life and dashed with difficulty; a way that is often misunderstood and requires a calculated cost. It's a path that scripture says "few find".

While this path may be costly, it is worth whatever the price because *He* is worth it. He deserves everything and more than we could possibly give Him. When we consider all that God has done for us, our natural response should be a surrendered life to Him; a steadfast and unwavering life devoted to knowing

Him and making Him known. No matter what our circumstances look like in any season of life, we can consistently choose Him. In the valleys and on the mountaintops, we live for Him.

One key to staying steadfast and resolved in our faith journey is found in Hebrews 12:1 - *let us lay aside every weight and the sin which so easily ensnares us, and let us run with endurance the race that is set before us.* We all have a race set before us, filled with plans and purposes created uniquely by God Himself. The enemy will want to throw weight and sin our way to slow us down or stop us completely from enduring the race; we must refuse to let him. We have the ability and authority to identify all weight and sin and to get rid of it so that we can continually move forward on the path that God has created for our lives.

This life is fleeting, temporary, and unpredictable. We are called for an eternal purpose, to set our minds on things above and to stay seated with Christ in Heavenly places. The Bible says that He fashions our days for us (Psalm 139). Look for Him in the ordinary as well as the extraordinary - He is found in both. 1 Corinthians 15:58 - *Therefore, my beloved brethren, be steadfast, immovable, always abounding in the work of the Lord, knowing that your labor is not in vain in the Lord.*

Ponder verses: Psalm 51:10; Psalm 136:26; Hebrews 3:14; Hebrews 6:18; James 1:17

Prayer:

Heavenly Father, thank You for Your steadfast, never-ending love for me. You are so faithful, and Your love endures forever. I choose the narrow path with You, God. I ask You to help me identify any weight or sin that keeps me from running my race well. I want it removed from my life so that I can do all that You've called me to without any hindrances. In Jesus' name, amen.

Wholehearted

"Then you will call upon Me and go and pray to Me, and I will listen to you. And you will seek Me and find Me when you search for Me with all your heart." - Jeremiah 29:12-13

We are called to live a life of passionate, fiery faith. Our commitment to God should be zealous and full of fervor. God isn't looking for half-hearted, divided attention; He longs for fidelity and a complete union of our heart and life with His. He holds nothing back from us, and we are to reciprocate with wholehearted, authentic devotion to Him.

We are instructed in scripture to search for and to trust Him with all of our heart. That means we leave nothing on reserve. With every fiber of our being, we look for and pursue Him, and He promises that when we do, He will be found. Fully trusting Him means maintaining complete confidence in Him, knowing that He is unfailingly reliable and forever faithful.

To know Him better, we must make time to scour through scriptures and be in His presence. He wants to reveal Himself to us, and Psalm 14:2 tells us that He is looking for those who are seeking Him. He knows when our heart's affections are set on Him, and He doesn't sit idly when He sees our hunger and pursuit of Him. James 4:8 says that when we draw near to God, He will draw near to us. He always acknowledges and responds to our pursuit of Him.

Peter, one of the original twelve disciples, displayed an influential life of following God. He not only abandoned everything to follow Jesus, but he exhibited an unusual eagerness to demonstrate his dedication. We find accounts of him bravely stepping out of a boat to walk on water with Jesus and later defending Him by chopping off the ear of a man who was arresting Him. Peter didn't always respond right to situations, but his heart was whole towards God, and Jesus chose him to be "the rock on which he would build the church" (Matthew 16:18).

When we live our lives in service to the Living King, we must always keep Him as our focus and motive. People will fail us, let us down, and disappoint us, but He never will. Jesus came to serve, and we are called to mimic the life He lived. Ephesians 6:7 says, "serve wholeheartedly as if you were serving the Lord, not men." We are told the same message in Colossians 3:23 - "whatever you do, do it heartily, as to the Lord and not to men." All that we do in love, we do for Him with our whole hearts.

Ponder verses: Psalm 103:1-2; Proverbs 3:5-6; Matthew 20:28; 1 Corinthians 16:14

Prayer:

Heavenly Father, thank You for keeping Your gaze on me. I choose to intentionally draw near to You and I know that You respond by drawing near to me. I pray that when You look for those that are searching for You, that You find me searching. I want to live my life in a way that honors and pleases You. I pray that I would serve You wholeheartedly all the days of my life and that I would serve others from a place of genuine love. In Jesus' name, amen.

Come Away With Me

"Can you not discern this new day of destiny breaking forth around you? The early signs of my purposes and plans are bursting forth. The budding vines of new life are now blooming everywhere. The fragrance of their flowers whispers, "There is change in the air." Arise, my love, my beautiful companion, and run with me to a higher place. For now, is the time to arise and come away with me." - Song of Songs 2:13 TPT

As long as we have breath in our lungs and a beat in our hearts, the invitation to come away with God is always open. We were created to intimately know the One who intricately created us. He is not aloof, unresponsive, and indifferent towards humanity. Psalm 145:18 proves His desire to be close to us - *The Lord is near to all who call upon Him, to all who call upon Him in truth*. When we call to Him, He responds with nearness.

Romans 1:20 says, "For since the creation of the world God's invisible qualities—his eternal power and divine nature—have been clearly seen, being understood from what has been made, so that people are without excuse.". God wants to be known, and He has made Himself known since the beginning of creation's existence. When sin separated us from Him, He made a way to restore the breach through the life, death, and resurrection of Jesus Christ.

Jesus spoke a parable about wise and foolish virgins to His followers with instructions for waiting readily for His return. In this parable, when the Bridegroom came for them, half of them were ready and able to enter the wedding. The other half were not prepared; the door was shut and unable to be opened. The Bridegroom's response was, "I do not know you." John 17:3 says, "this is eternal life, that they may know You, the only true God, and Jesus Christ whom You have sent." Eternal life begins the moment we are born-again, accepting God's free gift of salvation. It marks the beginning of a life journeyed hand-in-hand with Him.

God is calling us to return to our first love and to remember that we can intimately know the One who is already intimately acquainted with us. In His presence is fullness of joy, and where His Spirit is, there is freedom. Let Him pour His lavish love on you as you experience Him in deeper, more intimate ways than ever before. You are invited to come away with Him to the secret place, as frequently and for as long as you decide. He is beckoning you-come.

Ponder verses: Psalm 143:8; Matthew 25:1-13; 2 Corinthians 4:6; 1 Thessalonians 4:13-18

Prayer:
Heavenly Father, I say "yes" to Your invitation to come away with You. I desire to know You deeper than I ever have. I want

to live my life from an intimate relationship with You and to show others that knowing You is a beautiful way to live. I give my entire life to know You and to make You known. I ask You to direct my path and show me the plans You have for my life. I thank You for new days of destiny that are breaking forth around me. In Jesus' name, amen.

ABOUT KHARIS PUBLISHING

KHARIS PUBLISHING is an independent, traditional publishing house with a core mission to publish impactful books, and channel proceeds into establishing mini-libraries or resource centers for orphanages in developing countries, so these kids will learn to read, dream, and grow. Every time you purchase a book from Kharis Publishing or partner as an author, you are helping give these kids an amazing opportunity to read, dream, and grow. Kharis Publishing is an imprint of Kharis Media LLC. Learn more at https://www.kharispublishing.com.

www.ingramcontent.com/pod-product-compliance
Lightning Source LLC
Chambersburg PA
CBHW070157100426
42743CB00013B/2940